PROJECT AIR FORCE

T0293231

2017 U.S. Air Force Community Feedback Tool

Key Results Report for Air Force Headquarters

Carra S. Sims, Laura L. Miller, Thomas E. Trail, Dulani Woods, Aaron Kofner, Carolyn M. Rutter, Marek N. Posard, Owen Hall, Meredith Kleykamp

Prepared for the United States Air Force

Approved for public release; distribution unlimited

For more information on this publication, visit www.rand.org/t/RR3084

Library of Congress Cataloging-in-Publication Data is available for this publication.
ISBN: 978-1-9774-0382-7

Published by the RAND Corporation, Santa Monica, Calif.
© Copyright 2019 RAND Corporation
RAND® is a registered trademark.

Cover credits: Top: left, Tech. Sgt. Lealan Buehrer; middle, Tech. Sgt. Nadine Barclay; right, 2nd Lt. Brittany Curry.
Bottom: Airman 1st Class John Nieves Camacho; middle, Greg L. Davis; right, Master Sgt. John Nimmo, Sr., U.S. Air Force.

Support RAND
Make a tax-deductible charitable contribution at
www.rand.org/giving/contribute

www.rand.org

Preface

This report provides Air Force-level results from the 2017 Air Force Community Feedback Tool and documents the study methods. The web-based survey was administered in August and September 2017. All active, guard, and reserve airmen; their spouses; and Air Force civilian employees were eligible and invited to participate.

The top priority of the survey was to provide local commanders and service providers input from their own local Air Force communities about their most significant problems and needs. Thus, in April 2018, reports for internal Air Force use were provided for major active and reserve Air Force installations and guard wings and for additional installations where large numbers of airmen are stationed. The next set of reports, provided in May 2018, aggregated feedback across installations. These reports were prepared for all major commands and the Air Force District of Washington. In June 2018, results from guard members and guard spouses were provided to the Air National Guard.

This final report describes overall feedback from across the entire Air Force. The large sample sizes enable more-detailed analysis of differences across demographic subgroups and types of locations than was feasible at the installation or major command level.

The main purpose of this report is to highlight many key findings from the survey that could help inform the Community Action Plans of local Community Action Boards and Community Action Teams but not to provide an exhaustive catalog of all possible findings that could be derived from the survey. This goal was chosen after an Air Force comprehensive review of reports from previous community assessment surveys. The research team consulted with the sponsor to identify what types of key findings should be highlighted. Leaders and program staff can use data specific to their areas of responsibility to help make their programs, policies, and outreach efforts more effective or to confirm that what they have in place meet the population's needs.

The research reported here was commissioned by the commander of the Air Force Medical Operations Agency from May 2016 to May 2018, Brig Gen Robert I. Miller, on behalf of the Air Force Community Action Board. It was conducted within the Manpower, Personnel, and Training Program of RAND Project AIR FORCE as a part of a fiscal year 2016 project, "Air Force Comprehensive Needs Assessment."

RAND Project AIR FORCE

RAND Project AIR FORCE (PAF), a division of the RAND Corporation, is the U.S. Air Force's federally funded research and development center for studies and analyses. PAF provides the Air Force with independent analyses of policy alternatives affecting the development, employment, combat readiness, and support of current and future air, space, and cyber forces. Research is conducted in four programs: Strategy and Doctrine Force; Modernization and Employment; Manpower, Personnel, and Training; and Resource Management. The research reported here was prepared under contract FA7014-16-D-1000.

Additional information about PAF is available on our website: http://www.rand.org/paf/

This report documents work originally shared with the U.S. Air Force in April and September 2018.

Contents

Preface iii

Figures vii

Tables ix

Summary... xi

Acknowledgments xxiii

Abbreviations xxiv

1. Overview of Approach and Key Methodological Points 1
   Air Force Community Feedback Tool Objective...1
   Community Member Definitions 2
   Survey Recruitment and Administration..3
   Overall Air Force Population Characteristics and Response Rates 4
   Time to Complete the Survey..6
   Analytic Approach 7
   Constraints and Limitations 11
   Organization of This Report..15

2. Self-Rated Health and Resilience-Related Measures 17
   Exploring Variation in Responses: Limited-Activity Days and Perceived Resilience 23
   Findings and Conclusions 28

3. Self-Reported Problems and Needs in the Past Year 30
   Types of Problems: All and Sole or Most Significant 30
   Needs for Assistance with Top Problems 36
   Exploring Variation in Responses: Sole or Most Significant Type of Problem 45
   Findings and Conclusions 54

4. Help-Seeking Behaviors Among Respondents with Needs 57
   Resources Contacted for Greatest Needs 57
   Perceived Effectiveness of Resources Used..60
   Exploring Variation in Responses: Unmet Needs Among Those Who Reached Out for
      Assistance 69
   Findings and Conclusions 72

5. Community Feedback on Military Resources 74
   Perceived Attributes of Military Resources 74
   Ease or Comfort with Using Military Resources 78
   Perceived Impact of a Resource No Longer Being Available..80
   Preferred Means of Receiving Information About Services ...:..82
   Exploring Variation in Responses: Discomfort Using or Difficulty Finding Out About Military
      Resources 85

    Findings and Conclusions 87

6.   Attitudes Toward the Military 90
    Air Force Personnel Attitudes Toward Continuing Military Service or Employment...........90
    Personnel Beliefs About Their Spouse's or Partner's Support for Continuing Military Service or
        Employment..91
    Spouse's Attitudes Toward Their Airmen's Continuing Military Service 92
    Satisfaction with Military Life or Employment 93
    Airman and Spouse Satisfaction with How the Air Force Treats Them and Their Families.................94
    Exploring Variation in Responses: Satisfaction and Preference for Military Service or
        Employment..96
    Findings and Conclusions 101

7.   Correlations Between Key Indicators of Interest 103

8.   Key Findings, Conclusions, and Recommendations 107
    Key Findings and Conclusions..107
    Implications 112
    Recommendations for Further Data Analysis 112
    Recommendations to Respond to Community Feedback 113

Appendixes
A. Communities for Which Reports Were Prepared 116
B. Additional Methodological Details and Recommendations 121
C. Respondent and Location Characteristics...148
D. Specific Issues Experienced Within the Most Commonly Selected Top Problems 153
E. Integrated Health Summary 159

References 162

Figures

Figure S.1. Air Force Personnel's Top Type of Problem in the Past Year, Among Those with Any Problems xiii

Figure S.2. Air Force Spouses' Top Type of Problem in the Past Year, Among Those with Any Problems xiii

Figure S.3. Among Air Force Personnel Who Contacted a Resource for Help, Were Needs for Their Top Type of Problem Met? (%) xvi

Figure S.4. Among Spouses Who Contacted a Resource for Help, Were Needs for Their Top Type of Problem Met? (%) xvii

Figure 2.1. Air Force Personnel's Agreement That Each Characteristic Describes Their Social Support Networks, by Subgroup 20

Figure 2.2. Spouses' Agreement That Each Characteristic Describes Their Social Support Networks... 21

Figure 3.1. Air Force Personnel's Top Type of Problem in the Past Year, Among Those with Any Problems 33

Figure 3.2. Air Force Spouses' Top Type of Problem in the Past Year, Among Those with Any Problems 33

Figure 3.3. Air Force Personnel's Ratings of the Intensity of Their Top Type of Problem in the Past Year (%)... 35

Figure 3.4. Air Force Spouses' Ratings of the Intensity of Their Top Type of Problem in the Past Year (%)... 36

Figure 3.5. Among Air Force Personnel with Problems and Needs in the Past Year, All Self-Reported Needs for Their Top Type of Problem... 38

Figure 3.6. Among Spouses with Problems and Needs in the Past Year, All Self-Reported Needs for Their Top Type of Problem 39

Figure 3.7. Greatest Self-Reported Needs for Top Problem Types, Among Air Force Personnel Who Experienced a Problem in the Past Year............................... 40

Figure 3.8. Greatest Self-Reported Needs for Top Problem Types, Among Spouses Who Experienced a Problem in the Past Year 41

Figure 4.1. Air Force Personnel's Assessments of How Well Military Resources Contacted Were Able to Help with Greatest Needs for Their Top Type of Problem (%).....................62

Figure 4.2. Spouses' Assessments of How Well Military Resources Contacted Were Able to Help with Greatest Needs for Their Top Type of Problem (%) 63

Figure 4.3. Air Force Personnel's Assessments of How Well Nonmilitary Resources Contacted Were Able to Help with Greatest Needs for Their Top Type of Problem (%) 64

Figure 4.4. Spouses' Assessments of How Well Nonmilitary Resources Contacted Were
Able to Help with Greatest Needs for Their Top Type of Problem (%) 65

Figure 4.5. Among Air Force Personnel Who Contacted a Resource for Help, Were Needs
for Their Top Type of Problem Met? (%) 67

Figure 4.6. Unmet Needs Among Air Force Personnel Who Contacted a Resource for Help
with Their Top Problem, by Subgroup...68

Figure 4.7. Among Spouses Who Contacted a Resource for Help, Were Needs for Their
Top Type of Problem Met? (%) 69

Figure 5.1. Agreement with Ease or Comfort Using Military Resources, Among Air Force
Personnel (%) 79

Figure 5.2. Agreement with Ease or Comfort Using Military Resources, Among Spouses of
Airmen (%)...80

Figure 5.3. Perceived Impact If Military Resources Were No Longer Available to Help
Them or Their Families Address Problems, Among Air Force Personnel (%).....................81

Figure 5.4. Perceived Impact If Military Resources Were No Longer Available to Help
Them or Their Families Address Their Problems, Among Spouses (%) 82

Figure 5.5. How Air Force Personnel Would Like to Receive Information About Resources
Available to Help Them 84

Figure 5.6. How Spouses Would Like to Receive Information About Resources Available
to Help Them...85

Figure 6.1. Air Force Personnel's Attitudes About Leaving or Staying in Military Service or
Employment 91

Figure 6.2. Air Force Personnel's Perceptions of Their Spouses' or Partners' Attitudes
Toward Their Military Service or Employment...92

Figure 6.3. Spouse's Attitudes Toward Their Airmen Leaving or Staying in the Air Force 92

Figure 6.4. Air Force Personnel's Satisfaction with the Military Way of Life or Military
Employment 93

Figure 6.5. Spouses' Satisfaction with the Military Way of Life..94

Figure 6.6. Airmen's Satisfaction with Air Force Respect, Support, and Concern for Them
and Their Families..95

Figure 6.7. Spouse Satisfaction with Air Force Respect, Support, and Concern for Them
and Their Families (%)..96

Tables

Table 1.1. Air Force Subgroup Population, Respondents, and Response Rate 5

Table 1.2. Average Time in Minutes to Complete the Survey, by Subgroup 7

Table 1.3. Variables Used in Regression Analyses, by Subgroup 9

Table 2.1. Health-Related Quality-of-Life Indicators, by Subgroup...18

Table 2.2. Average Perceived Resilience Total Score Out of a Possible Score of 40,
    by Subgroup..22

Table 2.3. Overview of Characteristics Associated with Notable Differences in Airmen's
    Self-Reported Limited-Activity Days Due to Poor Health and Perceived Resilience
    Scores 25

Table 2.4. Overview of Characteristics Associated with Notable Differences in Spouse
    Self-Reported Limited-Activity Days Due to Poor Health and Perceived Resilience
    Scores 27

Table 3.1. Problem Types, with Examples of Specific Issues..31

Table 3.2. Types of Problems the Air Force Community Faced Over the Previous
    12 Months, by Air Force Status (%)..32

Table 3.3. Two Greatest Self-Reported Needs for the Top Three Types of Problems,
    Among Air Force Personnel with a Problem in the Past Year 42

Table 3.4. Two Greatest Self-Reported Needs for the Top Three Types of Problems,
    Among Spouses with a Problem in the Past Year 44

Table 3.5. Overview of Characteristics Associated with Notable Differences in Airmen's
    Top Type of Problem..48

Table 3.6. Overview of Characteristics Associated with Notable Differences in Spouses'
    Top Type of Problem..51

Table 3.7. Overview of Characteristics Associated with Notable Differences in Civilian
    Employees' Top Type of Problem 53

Table 4.1. Military Resources Community Members Contacted for Self-Reported
    Greatest Needs for Their Top Type of Problem, Among Those with Such Needs 59

Table 4.2. Nonmilitary Resources Community Members Contacted for Self-Reported
    Greatest Needs for Their Top Type of Problem, Among Those with Such Needs 60

Table 4.3. Overview of Characteristics Associated with Notable Differences in Unmet
    Needs for Top Past-Year Problem, Among Airmen Who Reached Out for Assistance 71

Table 5.1. Percentage of Air Force Personnel Who Agreed with Descriptions of Various
    Resources...75

Table 5.2. Percentage of Spouses Who Agreed with Descriptions of Various Resources............77

Table 6.1. Overview of Characteristics Associated With Notable Differences in Airmen's Satisfaction and Preference to Remain in the Military...98
Table 6.2. Overview of Characteristics Associated with Notable Differences in Spouses' Satisfaction and Support for Their Airmen to Remain in the Military...............................100
Table 7.1. Interrelationships Between Air Force Personnel's Responses to Key Indicators of Interest...104
Table 7.2. Interrelationships Between Spouses' Responses to Key Indicators of Interest..........105
Table B.1. Structure of the 2017 Air Force Community Feedback Tool 122
Table B.2. Characteristics Included in Survey Response Models for Air Force Personnel........133
Table B.3. Results from Nonresponse Models that Describe the Association Between Individual- and Installation-Level Characteristics and Air Force Personnel Survey Participation...136
Table B.4. Six Spouse Groups Used to Adjust Survey Response Rates in the Models for Spouses 141
Table B.5. Results from Nonresponse Models That Describe the Association Between Individual- and Installation-Level Characteristics and Spouse Survey Participation 143
Table C.1. Characteristics of Airman Survey Respondents 149
Table C.2. Characteristics of Respondents Who Are Air Force Civilian Employees.................150
Table C.3. Characteristics of Spouse Respondents Who Are Not Also Airmen.........................151
Table C.4. Characteristics of Respondents' Servicing Locations 152
Table D.1. Air Force Personnel Who Experienced Different *Military Practices and Culture* Problems in the Past Year 154
Table D.2. Air Force Personnel Who Experienced Different *Own Well-Being* Problems in the Past Year...155
Table D.3. Air Force Personnel Who Experienced Different *Work-Life Balance* Problems in the Past Year...156
Table D.4. Spouses Who Experienced Different *Own Well-Being* Problems in the Past Year 157
Table D.5. Spouses Who Experienced Different *Work-Life Balance* Problems in the Past Year 158
Table D.6. Spouses Who Experienced Different *Military Practices and Culture* Problems in the Past Year...158

Summary

Background and Purpose

Airmen, their families, and Air Force civilian employees face a range of personal and work-related challenges. Such challenges can include living far from base, being periodically deployed, and having to deal with competing demands on their time. To assist Air Force leaders in identifying and prioritizing the needs of their communities, the Air Force sponsored the 2017 Air Force Community Feedback Tool—a self-reported needs assessment of Air Force community members. Community members included in this survey were active, guard, and reserve airmen; their spouses; and Air Force civilian employees. The ultimate purpose of this assessment, according to Air Force Instruction 90-501, is to inform Community Action Board (CAB) Community Action Plans.[1] CABs are a forum for community leaders and representatives from diverse organizations to collaborate to identify community issues, and to develop plans to address these issues (see Air Force Instruction 90-501, 2013).

Drawing on community member responses from more than 88,000 Air Force personnel (airmen and employees) and spouses of airmen gathered from August to October 2017,[2] this report seeks to answer the following questions:

1. What were community members' perceptions of their well-being?
2. What problems did community members encounter over the course of the past year?
3. What needs were associated with their sole or most significant (or "top") type of past-year problem?
4. What were the help-seeking behaviors of the individuals with needs for their top past-year problem?
5. What was the general community level of awareness of and attitudes toward resources?
6. What factors were associated with unmet needs?
7. Were attitudes toward the military associated with perceived well-being, unmet needs, or difficulty finding out about military resources?
8. Which demographic subgroups and locations may have had a greater need for outreach or assistance?

More-detailed results—including methods and highlights from selected subgroup results—are provided in the body of this report.

We drew from the survey responses from members of the Air Force community to develop a set of recommendations about what actions the Air Force could take to better support community members.

---

[1] CABs were formerly known as Community Action Information Boards (CAIBs).

[2] Other community members, such as contractors, retirees, and members of other Services, are outside the scope of the 2017 survey.

What Were Community Members' Perceptions of Their Well-Being?

Regarding overall indicators of well-being, more than 55% of community members believed that their health is excellent or very good, with only 1 to 2% rating it poor. On average, the number of self-reported poor physical health days in the past month was 3.9 among Air Force personnel and 3.3 among spouses of airmen (who were not airmen themselves at the time of the survey), while the average number of self-reported poor mental health days in the past month was 3.4 among Air Force personnel and 4.5 among spouses of airmen. Community members reported that there were about two to three days in the past month when poor mental or physical health kept them from their usual activities, such as self-care, work, or recreation. Perceived resilience scores within the Air Force community in 2017 were similar to scores found in the general population and varied very little across demographic and military service characteristic subgroups. Out of a highest possible perceived resilience score of 40, Air Force personnel had an average score of 31.8, and spouses had an average score of 29.6. There is no standard set of discrete cutoff scores that distinguish vulnerable from resilient populations.

What Problems Did Community Members Encounter Over the Course of the Past Year?

About 10% of Air Force personnel and 8% of spouses reported experiencing no problems in the past year, but most community members did report facing challenges. Most commonly, community members indicated that their top problems related to (1) military practices and culture, (2) work-life balance, or (3) their own well-being, as shown in Figures S.1 and S.2. An examination of the most frequently selected issues that fell within each of these three categories revealed themes that could relate to work-life conflict: perceptions of poor leadership, challenges in managing competing commitments, finding enough time for self-care, and problems with sleep and stress.

Figure S.1. Air Force Personnel's Top Type of Problem in the Past Year, Among Those with Any Problems

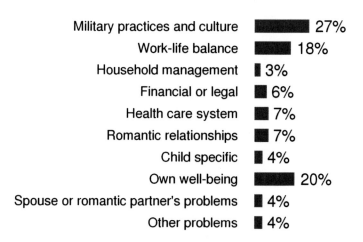

Military practices and culture 27%
Work-life balance 18%
Household management 3%
Financial or legal 6%
Health care system 7%
Romantic relationships 7%
Child specific 4%
Own well-being 20%
Spouse or romantic partner's problems 4%
Other problems 4%

NOTE: *N* = 71,247 personnel (airmen and Air Force civilian employees). *Top* refers to the sole type of problem experienced in the past year or to the type the respondent prioritized as most significant.

Figure S.2. Air Force Spouses' Top Type of Problem in the Past Year, Among Those with Any Problems

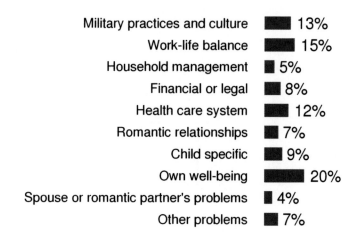

Military practices and culture 13%
Work-life balance 15%
Household management 5%
Financial or legal 8%
Health care system 12%
Romantic relationships 7%
Child specific 9%
Own well-being 20%
Spouse or romantic partner's problems 4%
Other problems 7%

NOTE: *N* = 6,708 spouses of airmen who are not airmen themselves. *Top* refers to the sole type of problem experienced in the past year or to the type the respondent prioritized as most significant.

What Needs Were Associated with Their Top Type of Past-Year Problem?

Survey participants who experienced any problems in the past year—about 90% of Air Force personnel and 92% of spouses—were asked to indicate what *kinds* of help they or their families needed to deal with the type of problem they had prioritized as most significant or as their only type of problem. Among community members who experienced problems in the past year, 40%

of Air Force personnel and 33% of spouses reported *not needing* assistance for their top type of problem. For those who did have a need, more commonly perceived types of need included advice, coaching, or education and general information (among personnel), and general information and emotional or social support (among spouses).

Among Air Force personnel dealing with military practices and culture problems, 18% needed general information; 16% indicated a need for advice, coaching, or education; and 14% wanted specific information. Similarly, among spouses dealing with military practices and culture problems, 27% needed specific information; 24% needed general information; and 10% believed that advice, coaching, or education would help them. These findings suggest that some of the solutions to military practices and culture problems may be relatively straightforward requirements related to better communication. However, solutions to other types of problems related to the demanding nature of Air Force work or perceptions of poor leadership may require more complex solutions.

What Were the Help-Seeking Behaviors of the Individuals with Needs for Their Top Past-Year Problem?

Not all community members who believed they needed help with their top type of problem reached out for assistance. Indeed, about 10% did not reach out to any military or nonmilitary resources. But community members who did reach out to military resources most often reported contacting the chain of command, other military coworkers or friends, or other military spouses for help, so having a chain of command and community well-informed of available resources is essential. Unfortunately, 29% of personnel and 34% of spouses who reached out to the chain of command reported that the contacts were "not at all" able to help with their greatest needs for their top problem. Some community members had concerns that reaching out to military health care resources or the chain of command could harm their or their spouses' or partners' reputations. But those who reached out to military mental health care providers or military chaplains or other members of a military religious or spiritual group were most likely to indicate these providers helped "a lot." Still, only 32% of personnel and 30% of spouses who contacted military mental health care providers felt they helped "a lot," and only 27% of personnel and 25% of spouses who contacted military chaplains or other members of a military religious or spiritual group felt they helped "a lot."

What Was the General Community Level of Awareness of and Attitudes Toward Military Resources?

The majority of personnel agreed that finding out about military resources is easy, that they are comfortable using those resources, and that they know who to contact if they have difficulty finding the right resources. However, a notable minority appeared to face challenges finding out about or being comfortable using resources. For airmen, having a heavy workload that required working long hours was associated with greater discomfort using or difficulty finding out about military resources, which could be related to lack of time in the day to do so. For spouses, being married to junior enlisted airmen and living farther from base (where many resources are advertised or located) was related to greater discomfort or difficulty. For civilian employees, those who were not also military veterans or current guard or reserve airmen felt greater discomfort using, or difficulty finding out about, military resources, which could be related to a relative lack of familiarity with (and eligibility for) the array of available resources due to less time and exposure to the military overall. Taken together, these findings suggest that the opportunity to become familiar with available resources when they are needed is key.

Spouses, in particular, may have difficulty finding out about military resources available to help them. Overall, only about one-half of spouses felt that finding out about military resources was easy, that they knew who to contact if they had a problem finding the right military resources for their needs, and that they were comfortable using the military resources available to them. Just over one-third of spouses reported knowing who to contact if military resources are not meeting their needs. More specifically, among guard spouses, 67% knew little to nothing about the guard's Family Assistance Center; among all spouses, 60% or more said they knew little to nothing about each of these resources: military hotlines or referral lines; resources for legal and policy violations; or support services for victims of violence, such as sexual assault or domestic violence. Moreover, between 50% and 59% of spouses were unfamiliar with each of the following resources: Air Force Key Spouse Program (whose mission is to support military spouses); Child and Youth Programs; military mental health care providers, and military chaplains or other members of military religious or spiritual groups. Although a continuous stream of new spouses requires orientation to Air Force and other military resources, these results suggest that more spouses need to be made aware of the resources available to support them and their families.

In terms of how personnel and spouses would like to receive information about resources available to help them (outreach), personnel tended to prefer unit leader emails sent to their Air Force email address, followed by a preference for leaders to send emails to their personal email address. Unit leaders sending emails to personal email addresses was also one of the top preferences among spouses. That preference for sending information to a personal email account makes particular sense for guard and reserve members who infrequently have access to their official Air Force email account (e.g., drill weekends) and for spouses who do not have an Air Force email account. Not everyone may be comfortable providing their personal email address to their or their spouses' chain of command or wish to receive official Air Force communication through both their personal and official email address, but, clearly, some actually preferred it over other forms of communication. Notably, installation newspapers and television announcements were among the least commonly preferred ways of receiving information about support services.

What Factors Were Associated with Unmet Needs?

We asked community members who reached out for help whether their needs were met for their top type of problem. Overall, 58% of Air Force personnel with at least one problem in the past year who contacted someone for assistance reported that, at the time of the survey, they had unmet needs, despite reaching out. Figure S.3 shows these results for Air Force personnel, by type of problem.

Figure S.3. Among Air Force Personnel Who Contacted a Resource for Help, Were Needs for Their Top Type of Problem Met? (%)

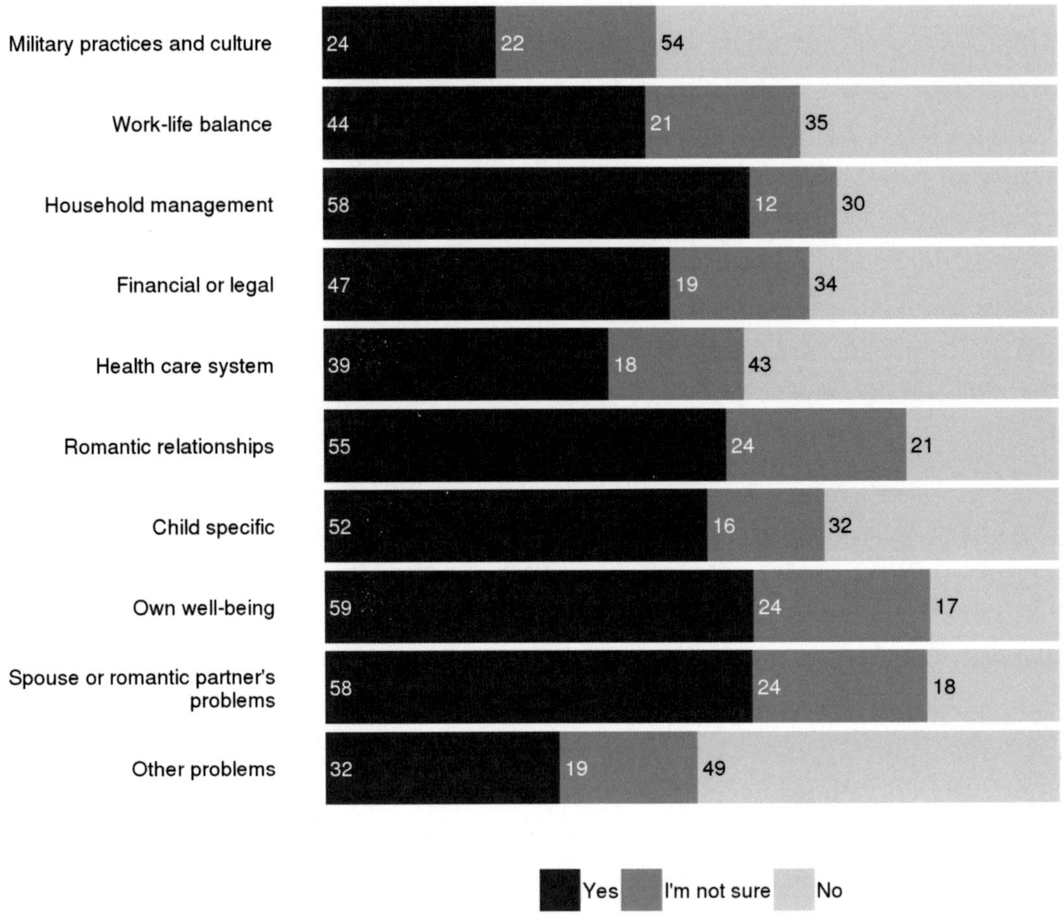

	Yes	I'm not sure	No
Military practices and culture	24	22	54
Work-life balance	44	21	35
Household management	58	12	30
Financial or legal	47	19	34
Health care system	39	18	43
Romantic relationships	55	24	21
Child specific	52	16	32
Own well-being	59	24	17
Spouse or romantic partner's problems	58	24	18
Other problems	32	19	49

NOTE: *N* = 35,897 personnel (across all rows in the figure). *Top* refers to the sole type of problem experienced in the past year or to the type the respondent prioritized as most significant. This figure includes only personnel who experienced problems in the past year, identified needs for their top type of problem, and reached out to at least one military or nonmilitary resource for assistance.

The majority of personnel whose top problem types were their own well-being, problems their spouse or romantic partner experienced, or household management indicated that their needs had been met (58–59%).

Similar types of problems were likely to be resolved for spouses (see Figure S.4): A majority of spouses indicated that their needs were met when their top problem type was their own well-being or household management (64% and 58%, respectively). However, only 45% reported that the needs for the problems their airmen experienced were resolved.

Figure S.4. Among Spouses Who Contacted a Resource for Help, Were Needs for Their Top Type of Problem Met? (%)

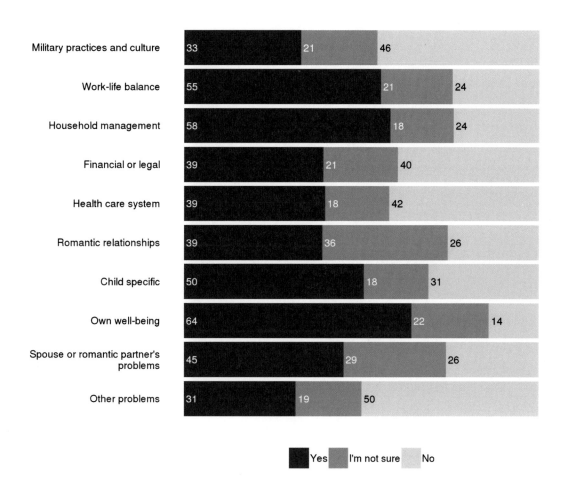

NOTE: *N* = 3,808 spouses. *Top* refers to the sole type of problem experienced in the past year or to the type the respondent prioritized as most significant.

More than one-half of personnel and spouses were able to find resources to help them resolve household management challenges (possible issues included needed home repairs, car repairs, or moving), which leaves a substantial minority with unmet needs in this area. Also, a notable minority of personnel and spouses (more than one-third) were not able to find resources to help them resolve problems relating to well-being—one of the more frequent top problem types. Frequently reported issues for well-being problems included trouble sleeping, feeling stressed and overwhelmed, and being frequently tired.

The problem type for which the highest proportion of personnel indicated unmet needs was for military practices and culture, at 76% (the combination of "No" and "I'm Not Sure" in Figure S.3). The most frequent problem type for which spouses reported not having their needs met after reaching out was also military practices and culture (67%; Figure S.4). As an example of the types of issues identified among those for whom this was their top problem, 59% of Air Force personnel indicated that one of the issues was poor leadership from the military chain of command. Additionally, 31% of personnel who reported that military practices and culture problems were their top problem in the past year indicated that, at its worst, this problem became severe.

For airmen, characteristics associated with unmet needs include living 30 or more minutes away from base and spending 180 or more nights in a given year away from home because of military duties, such as deployments, temporary duty, training, and field exercises. In addition to nights away from home, other aspects of heavy workload can also affect whether personnel get their needs met. The results suggest that both airmen and civilian employees who reported working 50 or more hours per week and the spouses of airmen who bear a similar workload appear to be particularly vulnerable.

Were Attitudes Toward the Military Associated with Perceived Well-Being, Unmet Needs, or Difficulty Finding Out About Military Resources?

Community members whose greatest needs for their top problem went unmet, despite reaching out for assistance in resolving their problem, reported a greater preference for leaving military service or employment than did those whose needs were met. For both airmen and their spouses, successful resolution of their top problem was associated with higher satisfaction with the military than was having unmet needs. Air Force personnel's perceptions of their own resilience was moderately associated with military satisfaction; this association was weak among spouses.

For both airmen and spouses, the measure of discomfort with using military resources or difficulty finding out about them was relatively strongly associated with lower satisfaction with military life and treatment of families.

Which Demographic Subgroups and Locations May Have Had a Greater Need for Outreach or Assistance?

Generally speaking, on selected indicators of interest (e.g., resilience measures, unmet needs) we found no evidence of major differences in responses from community members in remote or isolated locations, those serving in a foreign country, those serving on a non–Air Force–led installation, or those serving somewhere other than an installation (such as in recruiting stations, in Reserve Officer Training Corps units, or with another agency). Although our findings do not prove such characteristics are irrelevant, the findings do suggest that other characteristics were more influential.

Our findings in several areas highlight the benefits of experience with the system and resource availability. For example, those with more connections to the Air Force—such as veterans now serving as civilian employees or airmen and their spouses with more seniority—tended to be more comfortable using or better at finding out about military resources. More-senior personnel and those with spouses who work were also less likely to select such problems as financial and legal challenges as their top problem. However, more-senior personnel had problems, too. Both junior and senior officers were *more* likely than junior enlisted to indicate that work-life balance was a top type of problem in the past year, which could reflect more work-life conflict among officers, or that this problem type was more commonly noted simply because other problems (e.g., financial and legal) were less common.

Overall, however, these findings reinforce the potential greater or differing needs of particular groups—active component airmen, junior enlisted and their spouses, personnel who bear a heavy workload, and airmen and spouses that live farther from Air Force resources—and highlight the importance to the Air Force community of being able to successfully solve life's problems.

Our analyses prioritized topics or individual characteristics of particular concern to the sponsor or community leaders or hypothesized to hold particular relevance based on previous research. However, there are several other potential avenues for exploration. The Air Force may also wish to explore further whether perceived needs for community members vary by military service or demographic characteristics. In the current research, we examine whether the type of problem that was community members' top problem in the past year varied by characteristics. We recommend exploring further whether the perceived needs that correspond to these problems vary by such characteristics as location, demographics, or military service. For any particular topics or demographic subgroups the Air Force decides to prioritize, specific analyses could be run on the survey item about how these groups specifically would like to be contacted. These represent only some examples of the additional analyses the Air Force may find fruitful.

Recommendations: What Can the Air Force Do in Response to Community Feedback?

Looking across the answers to the seven questions, we offer some recommendations for moving forward related to the Air Force responding to the problems and needs in the community identified by the survey.

Pay special attention to the challenges associated with meeting the top three most frequently reported types of problem that the community felt mattered most. As discussed in our findings, military practices and culture, well-being, and work-life balance were the top three problem types identified. Particularly for airmen, the reported frequencies of these top problem types clearly rise above other problem types. Thus, Air Force initiatives targeted at resolving issues within these domains may be particularly likely to serve the communities. But the interventions may differ significantly for each type of problem. Some interventions needed may be relatively straightforward and may not require a change in policy or a new or revised program; for example, community members often believed that what they needed to deal with military practices and culture problems was information or advice. In such situations, improved information-sharing about plans and career opportunities and making sure military programs and services are accessible and known may be sufficient. However, some of the issues reported for this problem type, such as poor leadership, may be more difficult to manage and may need to be addressed through leadership training or professional military education.

Promote creative peer-to-peer information-sharing about available resources. Examples could include self-made videos, Instagram challenges, poster design contests, Twitter chats, scavenger hunts (e.g., locating different resources or providers)—popular but appropriate means of tapping into the creativity, energy, and social networks within the community. New approaches that engage user-generated social media content trends seem warranted by the lack of community awareness about many key resources; the difficulty some community members reported in finding out about resources; and the apparent tendency of so many community members to look to military coworkers, friends, and other military spouses for help with their needs. The Air Force can help facilitate brainstorming, enlisting volunteers, and providing the accurate and useful information to feed into the dissemination strategies.

Consider improvements in Air Force management of workload. Working 50 hours or more a week was associated with problems related to military practices and culture or work-life balance, more limited-activity days due to poor mental or physical health, greater discomfort using or difficulty finding out about military resources, and unmet needs despite reaching out for help. Leadership efforts for units with persistently heavy workloads could include reducing requirements, changing duties to facilitate working more efficiently, or increasing manpower. Installation leaders may not have the authority or resources to implement some of these changes, however, without support from higher levels of the organization. Also note that the workload may actually need to be increased in the short term to implement changes that lead to long-term workload reductions. For example, existing personnel may need to take on additional duties to train new personnel or to reorganize the workplace for more efficient workflow before some workload relief occurs. Thus, leaders, managers, and supervisors should be particularly attentive to the additional stress on the community during these transition periods. To truly achieve the desired benefits, leaders should resist the temptation to use any efficiencies gained to stretch the workload back to maximum capacity.

Reducing workload for officers who are persistently stretched thin may serve a dual purpose: It may also allow these leaders more time to meaningfully engage with their unit members and to respond more effectively when those in their charge turn to them for advice, information, or other types of assistance for their needs. However, if workload reductions are accompanied by expectations that officers will then be able to accommodate additional tasks, workloads may not be appreciably reduced.

Mine existing workload and manpower data. Workload and manpower data already available to the Air Force may reveal in more detail where airmen or employees need relief in terms of schedules, tasks, and staffing. Recent interviews with squadron commanders found that even units that appear to have sufficient manning may feel understaffed relative to required tasks (Ausink et al., 2018). Mining that data could help give the Air Force a better understanding of personnel needs.

Address sleep-related challenges through multiple avenues; reasons for insufficient or poor-quality sleep can vary. Many possible interventions are available to deal with the different types of sleep-related challenges that community members commonly reported. A variety of circumstances can contribute to sleep-related issues, such as heavy work demands or shift work, personal life stressors, behaviors (e.g., too much caffeine, electronics at bedtime), environmental issues (e.g., noise, temperature), and mental or physical health. A recent joint consensus statement of the American Academy of Sleep Medicine and Sleep Research Society asserts that, "Adults should sleep *7 or more* hours per night on a regular basis to promote optimal health" (Watson et al., 2015, p. 591; emphasis in the original). We echo recommendations from recent RAND Corporation research on sleep in the military (Troxel et al., 2015), which are still current and applicable here:

- **Across the community:** *Promote efforts to improve sleep hygiene, time management, and stress management* through multiple strategies, such as screening, coaching, instruction, apps, and information campaigns. Where personnel are routinely required to work 50 or more hours a week, these strategies should complement leadership efforts to reduce workplace stress and persistently heavy workloads, not substitute for them.
- **Among leaders:** *Educate line leaders on the value of sleep and how to address cultural and environmental barriers to healthy sleep,* including providing background on the consequences of poor sleep for performance, safety, decisionmaking, and mental and physical health.
- **Among health care professionals:** Ensure providers are educated on how to screen for, prevent, and treat sleep disorders.

Facilitate outreach through email announcements. Given the outreach preferences community members expressed, it may be worthwhile to provide opportunities more systematically to opt in or subscribe to having announcements sent to their personal email addresses to inform them about new programs or provide them with information about existing programs. This may be particularly useful for reaching guard and reserve members and spouses who are not civilian employees or airmen themselves.

Conduct follow-on efforts to better understand perceptions of poor leadership. Among personnel whose top problem was military practices and culture, about 60% believed that the military personnel in their chain of command provided poor leadership. This finding represents a starting point for action, but detailed local context would be useful for change initiatives at the local level (i.e., those that do not suggest Air Force–level policy involvement). Such local information could be collected at town halls, through focus groups, through solicitation of input via dropboxes, through outreach by chaplains and first sergeants, and through a review of Total Force Climate Survey results. Sharing local findings with Air Force headquarters may reveal more widespread leadership quality issues that should be channeled to organizations that manage professional development, career assignments, promotion decisions, or leadership screening and selection processes.

Acknowledgments

Maj Mark Oliver provided project oversight and guidance on the survey instrument, survey marketing materials, templates for the tailored reports prepared for the communities listed in Appendix A and for the analytic approach for the analyses described in this report. Representatives from across the Air Force also offered advice on prioritization and communication of the survey items and results. Maj Jordan Simonson at the Air Force Personnel Center and Daniel Perkins and Kristin Brawley at the Clearinghouse for Military Family Readiness provided helpful reviews of the report templates, which were also applicable to this final report. Nicholas Ruther and Benjamin Phillips at Abt Associates provided invaluable support in the programming and administration of the survey. Hla Myint at the Air Force Medical Operations Agency staffed the Air Force helpdesk for the survey and offered input on the survey instrument, survey template, and a draft of this survey report.

At RAND, the report text benefited from copyediting by Phyllis Gilmore and Jerry Sollinger. Jerry Sollinger and Paul Steinberg assisted with the drafting of the executive summary. Dori Walker improved the design of the figures. Elizabeth Coppola assisted as a quality control reviewer for both the survey instrument and the report template. Bernard Rostker assisted with the development of the installation report template. James Gazis created the survey information website; Christine Sovak designed the survey recruitment images; and Chara Williams assisted with both. Seifu Chonde and Ricardo Sanchez assisted in creating the computer program that tailored the results to each community and generated the reports. Perry Firoz managed the Air Force personnel data and survey access codes and supported survey invitation efforts. The work also benefited greatly from RAND management and quality assurance reviewers Kirsten Keller, Sarah Meadows, Kimberly Hepner, Matthew Cefalu, and Chaitra Hardison, as well as guidance from Ray Conley, David Orletsky, and Roald Euller. Additional RAND staff assisted in quality control checks, including Alexis Levedahl and Amy Grace Donohue.

Abbreviations

AFI	Air Force Instruction
AFSO	Air Force Survey Office
AUC	area under the curve
CAC	Common Access Card
CAB	Community Action Board (formerly the Community Action Information Board)
CD-RISC	Connor-Davidson Resilience Scale
CI	confidence interval
CoC	chain of command
DoD	U.S. Department of Defense
DMDC	Defense Manpower Data Center
DRU	direct reporting unit
MAJCOM	major command
NCO	noncommissioned officer
NR	not reportable
OPA	Office of People Analytics
ROTC	Reserve Officer Training Corps
SD	standard deviation
TV	television

1. Overview of Approach and Key Methodological Points

Airmen, their families, and Air Force civilian employees face a range of personal and work-related challenges. Such challenges can include living far from base, being periodically deployed, and having to deal with competing demands on their time. To assist Air Force leaders in identifying and prioritizing the needs of their communities, the Air Force sponsored the 2017 Air Force Community Feedback Tool—a self-reported needs assessment of Air Force community members. Community members included in this survey were active, guard, and reserve airmen; their spouses; and Air Force civilian employees. The ultimate purpose of this assessment, according to Air Force Instruction (AFI) 90-501, is to inform Community Action Board (CAB) Community Action Plans.[3] CABs are a forum for community leaders and representatives from diverse organizations to collaborate to identify community issues and to develop plans to address the issues (see AFI 90-501, 2013).

This chapter describes the objectives and the survey and research questions that guided this report, defines the community members eligible to participate, provides an overview of survey recruitment and administration, and reports population and response rates and the average amount of time participants devoted to completing the survey. It also provides an overview of our approach to analyzing the survey data, including statistical methods and criteria for determining which results to highlight in this report. Finally, the chapter outlines the limitations of the survey methods, analyses, and reporting and offers an overview of the structure of the remainder of this report. Methodological details (on such topics as the survey framework, survey recruitment and marketing, survey incentives, survey mode, analyses of nonresponse, and development of survey weights) appear in Appendix B.

Air Force Community Feedback Tool Objective

Air Force community members—airmen, their families, and Air Force civilian employees—may face complex and diverse challenges. Community input can help Air Force leaders prioritize resources and services to ensure that available support services are both needed and effective. The objective of the 2017 Air Force Community Feedback Tool was to provide a self-reported needs assessment of active, guard, and reserve airmen; their spouses; and Air Force civilian employees.[4] The ultimate purpose of this assessment, according to AFI 90-501, is to inform CAB Community Action Plans. CABs are a forum for community leaders and representatives from

---

[3] CABs were formerly known as Community Action Information Boards (CAIBs).

[4] *Self-reported needs assessment* refers to individuals reporting their own perceptions of what they need, in contrast to the type of needs assessment a health care professional might conduct to determine a recommended treatment plan.

diverse organizations (e.g., medical, legal, chaplain, manpower) to collaborate to identify community issues that may relate to readiness, retention, resilience, and quality of life and to develop plans to address these issues (AFI 90-501, 2013).

This report addresses the following research questions:

1. What were community members' perceptions of their well-being?
2. What problems did community members encounter over the course of the past year?
3. What needs were associated with their sole or most significant (or "top") type of past-year problem?
4. What were the help-seeking behaviors of the individuals with needs for their top type of past-year problem?
5. What was the general community level of awareness of and attitudes toward military resources?
6. What factors were associated with unmet needs?
7. Were attitudes toward military service or employment associated with perceptions of well-being, unmet needs, or difficulty finding out about military resources?
8. Which demographic subgroups and locations may have had a greater need for outreach or assistance?

Based on the answers provided by members of the Air Force's community, we provide a set of recommendations about what actions the Air Force could take to better support community members.

Appendix A provides complete lists of installations that are servicing locations for Air Force personnel and of the direct reporting unit (DRU) and major commands (MAJCOMs) that are responsible for those locations. Differences between feedback from community members in any particular community and the overall Air Force may stem from the specific demographics and installation characteristics rather than from differences in quality of personnel or community support. Thus, in this report, we will explore whether such differences exist for selected survey items.

Community Member Definitions

This report uses the following definitions for specific segments of the U.S. Air Force community, all of whom were eligible and invited to participate in this survey:

- **Active:** All active component Air Force military personnel. Includes airmen married to other airmen. Does not include guard and reserve members serving on active duty.
- **Guard and reserve:** All Air National Guard or Air Force Reserve military personnel, regardless of active duty status. Includes guard and reserve airmen who are also Air Force civilian employees or married to airmen.
- **Civilian employee:** All Air Force civilian employees, part time or full time, appropriated fund and nonappropriated fund. Includes civilian employees who are also guard or reserve airmen. Includes civilian employees who are also married to airmen.
- **Air Force personnel:** Refers collectively to the active, guard, and reserve airmen and civilian employees, as defined here.

- **Spouse:** Spouses of Air Force active, guard, or reserve military personnel who are not also Air Force active, guard, or reserve themselves. Includes spouses who are also Air Force civilian employees. For methodological reasons, these spouse results could not be combined and reported with results from airmen and civilian employees.[5]

Individuals who hold more than one of the above Air Force affiliations are not counted more than once in any combined results. However, to assist leaders and service providers focused on certain demographic subgroups, subgroup results may include individuals holding multiple statuses. For example, where subgroup results for guard members are reported, guard respondents may include individuals who are also married to other airmen or who are also civilian employees. It was not possible in time for this survey to obtain permission to include community members from other service branches serving on Air Force–led installations.

Survey Recruitment and Administration

The online survey was open from August 3 to October 9, 2017, to all active, guard, and reserve airmen; spouses of airmen; and Air Force civilian employees (a census). The survey was hosted on a .com website that did not require a U.S. Department of Defense (DoD) Common Access Card (CAC) smartcard, military computer, or military computer network for access. Both targeted messages and broad announcements invited community members to participate. Marketing efforts (e.g., messages on Air Force websites and social media) were one strategy for raising awareness about the survey, inviting participation, providing the survey information website address, and reminding community members throughout the survey administration period that the survey was underway.

For more-direct appeals, the Air Force Survey Office (AFSO) sent initial, personalized email invitations to the Air Force email addresses for all active, guard, and reserve airmen and civilian employees at the beginning of August 2017. The emails from an af.mil address indicated that AFSO was sending them on behalf of the Assistant Vice Chief of Staff of the Air Force and were digitally signed to assure recipients that the Air Force itself sent them. This strategy was also important for minimizing the likelihood that these mass emails would be blocked by security or junk email filters. The invitations included a link to the online survey and an individual survey access code, as well as a link to the survey information website and a link to the AFSO list of approved surveys. Invitations were timed to arrive just before or during the first weekend of the month, when many guard and reserve personnel would be coming to their duty stations for their

---

[5] Specifically, because the Air Force personnel files do not identify which civilian employees are also spouses of airmen and do not provide the characteristics of their airmen, we had to take a different approach to weighting these dual-status participants. Ultimately, we had to report their results separately to avoid double counting them.

monthly drills and have access to their Air Force email accounts. AFSO sent survey reminder emails at the beginning and end of September 2017.[6]

At the beginning of August 2017, postcards for spouses announcing the survey and providing survey access codes were mailed to the home addresses of married airmen.[7] In an effort to improve survey response rates, spouses were offered token incentives for survey participation (a $2 Amazon gift code), and approximately one-third of spouse respondents did request and receive this incentive. Because of legal restrictions and other concerns, airmen and employees were not offered incentives. Appendix B provides additional details on survey recruitment and administration and on recommendations for future efforts.

Overall Air Force Population Characteristics and Response Rates

This section provides a demographic snapshot of the overall Air Force population, based on Air Force personnel database information as of July 2017, immediately prior to the August launch of the survey.[8] Table 1.1 provides the number of Air Force community members by affiliation: active, guard, reserve, civilian employees, and spouses of airmen. It also shows the number of respondents and the response rates for those same demographic subgroups. Note that the totals are not the sums of the subgroups because some individuals hold more than one affiliation.

Survey Response Rates and Weights

All active, guard, and reserve airmen; their spouses; and Air Force civilian employees were eligible and invited to participate in the 2017 Air Force Community Feedback Tool. By survey *response rate*, we simply mean the number of survey participants who completed the initial sections of the survey (i.e., key demographics and problems they may have experienced in the past year) divided by the population sizes provided in Table 1.1, which reflect all Air Force personnel and the spouses of all married airmen (with exceptions as noted in footnote 8) as of July 2017. Across the Air Force as a whole, 88,592 individuals provided feedback to the Air Force through this tool, representing 13% of Air Force personnel and 3% of spouses.

---

[6] The magnitude of emails and digital signing meant the process of sending these emails was very resource intensive and took a few days to complete. Because of the resource constraints at AFSO and the labor required to send the emails, AFSO was unable to send more frequent reminders; however, the reminders AFSO was able to send did boost the number of responses obtained.

[7] AFSO does not have direct contact information for spouses, and the process for obtaining them from DoD would have extended beyond the Air Force's desired time frame for a survey launch, so emails to spouses were not part of the recruiting strategy this time.

[8] The data set the Air Force Personnel Center provided omitted personnel in a gain or dropped-from-rolls status (separated, retired, ready or standby reserve) or on duty statuses indicating they were patients, prisoners, parolees, or absent from the force (e.g., missing, absent without leave). Airmen who were students were included.

Table 1.1. Air Force Subgroup Population, Respondents, and Response Rate

	Air Force Population	Number of Respondents	Response Rate (%)
Air Force personnel	637,831[a]	81,833	13
Active component	309,567	41,286	13
Air National Guard	104,271	10,019	10
Air Force Reserve	69,785	5,063	7
Civilian employees	167,406	27,075	16
Spouses of airmen (who are not also airmen themselves)	227,397	7,434	3
Total	Unknown[a]	88,592[b]	Unknown[a]

SOURCE: July 2017 Air Force personnel files.

[a] These are unknown because the Air Force does not record whether civilian employees are also spouses of airmen, so we cannot determine the degree of overlap between these two populations.

[b] Not the sum of each subgroup because some individuals hold more than one Air Force affiliation.

Low response rates can be a concern if those who do participate in a survey differ in important ways from those who do not (*nonresponse bias*). However, there is no set scientific standard for a minimal response rate for a survey to be valid, or to designate it as representative or free from nonresponse bias. DoD survey response rates have been trending downward, as have survey participation rates more generally (Office of People Analytics [OPA], 2018e; Miller and Aharoni, 2015; National Research Council, 2013). Strategies to increase response rates, such as mailing paper survey follow-ups, can be costly, and the increased response may not "significantly or meaningfully chang[e] estimates from the survey" (U.S. Government Accountability Office, 2010, p. 6, citing a military-specific example). At the same time, empirical assessments of survey research have been finding that "the response rate of a survey may not be as strongly associated with the quality or representativeness of the survey as had been generally believed" (Johnson and Wislar, 2012, p. 1805; see also Groves, 2006; Groves and Peytcheva, 2008).[9]

Because the Air Force Community Feedback Tool is designed to provide results at the installation level, it is more important for this survey to obtain a large number of respondents than it is for some other surveys, which provide Air Force results overall rather than by location. **The large number of participants in the 2017 Air Force Community Feedback Tool reflects a relatively low percentage of respondents because the entire Air Force population was invited to participate.**

This report may not communicate all views that exist in the community but does represent the input of the many community members who were willing, able, and sufficiently motivated to engage Air Force leadership through this feedback tool. All survey responses presented in the

---

[9] Interested readers should refer to Appendix B for more information on response rates.

subsequent chapters of this report are adjusted, or "weighted," to account for observed differences in the characteristics of survey respondents relative to the overall Air Force population, which is also a standard practice for DoD surveys. More information about survey response rates and technical details about how the results are adjusted appear in Appendix B, as do recommendations for improving levels of survey participation in the future.

Minimum Sample Sizes for Reporting

To protect respondent confidentiality and avoid reporting of potentially imprecise results, this report displays results only when ten or more participants responded to the question and when 20 or more individuals in the population were potentially eligible to answer the question. At the Air Force level of reporting, this was not a challenge. Because of rounding, percentages may not sum to 100.

Time to Complete the Survey

The survey was designed with consideration for the amount of time it might take to participate. The predecessor to this survey, the 2013 Community Assessment Survey, took approximately one hour to complete on average (Dixon and Bares, 2018, p. 44). For the 2017 Air Force Community Feedback Tool, the Air Force wanted us to develop an instrument that would require a significantly shorter response time (in addition to accomplishing other goals).

A number of factors could influence time to completion. It will depend, in part, on how quickly respondents read items and whether they were interrupted or are multitasking. Completion time will also depend on how many survey items were presented. Those holding multiple Air Force statuses (e.g., civilian employee and spouse of airmen) will see more questions and response options than those holding only one. Additionally, those who experienced problems in the past year will see follow-up questions about whether or how they addressed any needs that may have resulted from past-year problems. Respondents who were interrupted during the survey were able to return later to finish.

To understand how much time community members devoted to survey participation, we analyzed the time stamps embedded in the survey programming. Our calculations included individuals who provided sufficient information to be counted as a respondent, regardless of whether they reached the final survey section. We summed the seconds spent on each survey section, including the introduction and consent. This method helped us to exclude some of the gaps for respondents who had started the survey on one day, were interrupted, and eventually logged back in to complete it some days or weeks later, although it does not exclude respondents who may have had the survey open for some time but were not actively engaged. Overall, 93% of the personnel surveys and 97% of the spouse surveys in our analytic data set were completed in two or fewer hours.

Table 1.2 shows the median survey completion time, by subgroup. These results show that the instrument came within its goal of taking less than 30 minutes to complete.

Table 1.2. Average Time in Minutes to Complete the Survey, by Subgroup

	Active	Guard	Reserve	Employee	Personnel Overall	Spouses of Airmen
Average number of minutes	23	22	22	21	22	21

NOTE: Responses from individuals who are both airmen and employees are included in both subgroups' results. Responses from civilian employees who are also spouses of airmen are included in both subgroups' results.

Analytic Approach

This report contains descriptive analyses in the form of means and percentages. The purpose of this study was to help the Air Force understand the community's needs and, ideally, what steps it might take to help members mitigate the challenges to facilitate a more ready and resilient community. Many of the findings of interest reside in a basic assessment of the types of problems and needs present in the community and the resources sought by community members to solve their challenges. The findings are presented here to provide an understanding of these concerns for the Air Force as a whole. To this end, as described above, these descriptive statistics are weighted to account for observed differences in the characteristics of survey respondents relative to the overall Air Force population. More information about these adjustments can be found in Appendix B. These descriptive analyses are presented at the beginning of each chapter, and chapters are grouped thematically. Because of the large number of respondents, significance tests between these major subgroups would tend to show statistically significant differences that could be based on sample size alone and that would not have meaningful or practical value for the Air Force (e.g., where there is only a 1-percentage-point difference between groups). Thus, testing for statistical significance across the descriptive analyses was not a priority over other opportunities for analysis.

The Air Force also seeks to understand whether survey responses were associated with either individual or location characteristics that could help leadership identify groups that might be vulnerable or groups that were doing particularly well. To answer these questions, we used regression analyses. The following were the key indicators of interest selected for this additional level of analysis, which we describe more fully in the relevant chapters:

- limited-activity days in the past month because of poor physical or mental health
- perceived resilience
- sole or most significant type of problem in the past year
- unmet needs associated with the top type of past-year problems, despite having reached out for assistance
- discomfort using or difficulty finding out about military resources

- satisfaction with military life and how the Air Force treats airmen and their families
- preference to leave military service or employment (turnover intentions).

These analyses offer the benefit of controlling for multiple location and demographic characteristics at once, so findings of significant differences in these analyses indicate group differences are significant, controlling for other factors in the regression model. Each of Chapters 2 through 6 first provides the descriptive results for a broader range of items, then concludes by presenting the regression results for the key indicators of interest.[10]

We estimated separate models for airmen, civilian employees, and spouses of airmen, meaning that we looked at relationships between respondent characteristics and item outcomes within these groups. Because personnel are not randomly geographically distributed (e.g., some locations may have higher concentrations of junior enlisted airmen or married personnel), our models simultaneously included both location and individuals' demographic and military service characteristics.

We also explored whether responses were correlated across these items (e.g., whether individuals who reported high perceived resilience also reported high degrees of comfort using or ease of finding military resources to meet their needs) and reported those in Chapter 7.

Variables Used in Statistical Models

Table 1.3 shows the location, military service, and demographic variables included in the regression models as predictors. As shown in Table 1.3, different information was available across the three populations. The characteristics chosen to include in regression models for each item were guided by both theoretical and practical considerations. For each item, we used similar sets of characteristics for airmen, civilian employees, and spouses of airmen, with some modifications pertinent to each population (e.g., military career group for airmen and employee type for employees).

We explored the potential relevance of location for two reasons. For outreach and program-planning purposes, Air Force leaders may wish to know *where* there may be greater need or different types of needs so that initiatives can be tailored appropriately. Additionally, location characteristics related to members' proximity to friends, family, Air Force resources, and the Air Force community may contribute to observed variation in responses.

Military service characteristics also have the potential to be relevant for community attitudes and experiences because they can represent tenure and position within the hierarchy, level of familiarity and interaction with the Air Force, work environment (e.g., because it may differ by career group), and the degree to which the demands of Air Force duties may compete with time for friends, family, or self-care. Marital status, having minor children, and employment status among spouses are also characteristics that could influence individuals' perceptions of their well-

---

[10] For technical readers, output with full model results is available from the authors.

being, the types of the problems they might experience, their ability to meet their and their families' needs, and their satisfaction with military life or employment.

More details about these variables and corresponding frequencies for these and other characteristics are provided in Appendix C.

Table 1.3. Variables Used in Regression Analyses, by Subgroup

		Airman	Civilian Employee	Spouses of Airmen[a]
Location	U.S. or foreign	✓	✓	✓
	Remote and isolated[b]	✓	✓	✓
	Non–Air Force–led installation	✓	✓	✓
	Somewhere other than an installation	✓	✓	✓
Military service	Component	✓		✓
	Dual hat: both airman and employee		✓	
	Rank group[c]	✓		✓
	Employee type		✓	
	Military career group	✓		
	Distance from base	✓	✓	✓
	Personnel nights away from home	✓		✓
	Personnel hours working Air Force duties	✓	✓	✓
	Veteran status		✓	
Demographic	Marital status	✓	✓	(All married)
	Minor child(ren)	✓	✓	✓
	Spouse employment			✓

[a] In the spouse models, component, rank group, nights away from home, and hours working refer to their airmen's characteristics.
[b] *Remote and isolated* is defined in AFI 65-106's guidance on the allocation of funds for such resources as morale, welfare, and recreational programs (2009, p. 14).
[c] Not asked of spouses who are also civilian employees.

For use in some of our models, we created a variable called "problem-solving status" to represent where respondents fell along the problem-solving continuum: Did they or did they not experience problems, have subsequent needs for assistance, or contact resources for help? And if they did make contact, were their needs met? Specifically, problem-solving status is based on survey responses across a series of questions that were used to sort respondents into one of nine categories:

- indicated no problems in the past year
- problems, but skipped follow-up questions
- problems and needs, but skipped follow-up questions
- problems but perceived no needs for their top problem
- problems and needs, but never contacted resources for assistance and did not indicate why

9

- problems and needs, but did not contact resources because their problems were resolved
- problems and needs, but did not contact resources for some other reason (such as lack of information about who to contact)
- problems and needs that were resolved through use of resources
- problems and needs that were not resolved through resources (unmet needs).[11]

This categorical variable was included as a predictor in regression models to explore how the problem-solving behaviors documented by the survey were related to key indicators of interest. For example, the models examined whether service members' attitudes toward the Air Force were associated with whether individuals experienced any problems or had any needs associated with their problems that were not resolved by accessing resources. Because this variable represented the problem-solving process the survey was assessing, the causal relationship between this variable and indicators of interest that also assessed aspects of the coping or problem-solving process is unclear. Thus, we did not include the problem-solving status variable in all models but only in models examining more distal concepts, such as attitudes toward the Air Force.[12] However, we did explore the association between an outcome of the problem solving process—whether or not respondents had unmet needs—and other problem-solving variables, such as resilience and comfort with military resources (see Chapter 7).

It was not feasible within the scope of this research to explore all possible variables of interest (e.g., gender, race, ethnicity). Therefore, this report focuses on key analyses that would be generally informative, focusing on items most likely to be important from a policy perspective, items that had proven useful in prior research, and items of particular interest to the Air Force. We encourage further data exploration to better understand the needs of Air Force populations.

Criteria for Significance, Both Statistical and Practical

Given the large number of survey respondents from across the Air Force, we anticipated that statistical tests of differences between demographic subgroups or locations based on the widely accepted 0.05 significance level would identify many very small but statistically significant differences between subgroups or locations that would not have practical value in terms of

---

[11] Some of these problem-solving status categories contained relatively few respondents (particularly in the case of the smaller population of spouses. For this group, the smallest category retained for analysis was the 61 spouses who had a top problem but provided no further information. Because we did not have empirical justification for how best to consolidate some of these categories, we retained even the smaller ones for analysis.

[12] Specifically, we did not include this variable in regression models for perceived resilience or comfort with resource use because both of these concepts may themselves be associated with how problem solving is approached: Resilience may be seen as an outcome of successful problem-solving but also could be a perception that would affect how people approached their problems and how willing they were to perceive resources available and reach out to them. Similarly, comfort using military resources or difficulty finding out about them could affect the approach to the problem-solving process (e.g., whether and what kind of resources were sought to help with problems).

guiding Air Force decisionmaking. For example, it is unlikely that the Air Force would wish to act on a 1-percentage-point difference in the frequency of the reported top problem in active component and reserve component airmen. Furthermore, because this report includes a large number of statistical tests, it likely that some of these tests will have statistically significant differences by chance alone.[13] To mitigate both issues related to policy relevance and multiple testing, we evaluated the results using two standards.

First, we set the criterion for statistical significance at $p < 0.001$ rather than the standard $p < 0.05$. This sets a higher bar for significant results and helps limit the number of statistically significant findings that might occur by chance alone.[14]

Second, we defined meaningful differences between subgroups or locations that reflect real-world practical differences between them that might merit further consideration for policy changes, based on each dependent variable, as appropriate. This approach aligns with guidance from the American Statistical Association warning against overreliance on p-values, asserting that "[n]o single index should substitute for scientific reasoning" (Wasserstein and Lazar, 2016, p. 132). For example, for unmet needs, we highlighted potentially meaningful differences in the odds ratios by setting a minimum odds ratio corresponding to a minimum percentage point difference of 5% as a threshold. For differences in 5-point scale items (e.g., 1-to-5 response scales or averages across multiple scale items), the minimum difference we chose to highlight was 0.25 scale point because this could represent a change in direction of the categorization of the response (e.g., from the "neither agree nor disagree" category to the "agree" category). Minimum differences are specified within each result discussion.

Constraints and Limitations

The 2017 Air Force Community Feedback Tool gathered a wealth of data from a large number of respondents who took the time to provide their feedback to Air Force leadership. In the following subsections, we offer for consideration some constraints of this research and limitations of the results that readers should keep in mind when interpreting them.

Survey Methods

The survey did not include non–Air Force civilian employees or members of other services who work on Air Force–led installations or rely on Air Force–led resources, and thus may also be considered part of the Air Force community. It takes much longer than the survey timeline

---

[13] Using a 0.05 significance level means that there is a 5% chance of finding a statistically significant difference when one does not exist. That is, we would expect 5 out of 100 tests to be statistically significant, even when there are no real differences.

[14] We used this ad hoc approach, rather than a Bonferroni correction for multiple comparisons, because we did not know how many tests we would take at the outset, and we could not naturally group tests into families of tests that could be used for correction.

allowed to obtain permissions to survey such a wide range of populations covered by different types of laws and policies.

This survey is cross-sectional: It asks participants at a single point in time to reflect on past-year problems. Perceptions of events may change over time, and recall may be imperfect, particularly for events that were further in the past.

The survey was not designed to provide a snapshot of problems current at the time of the survey. It was intended to provide a snapshot of individuals' interpretation of and responses to their past-year problems and whether any perceived needs were met.

To limit the survey length and thereby promote survey participation, respondents were asked follow-up questions about problems only for the sole or most significant type of problem they experienced in the past year. This strategy also helps leaders and service providers focus on their community's top issues. One trade-off, however, is that the survey does not capture unmet needs across the full range of problem types experienced.

Survey Participation

A large number of community members participated in the survey (88,592), and this level of feedback is certainly worthy of leaders' consideration. Nevertheless, the *percentage* of the Air Force community that participated was low (13% of personnel, 3% of spouses). It is possible that some types of experiences or views are insufficiently represented in our analyses, though it is worth noting this could also be true even if participation rates were higher. As noted above, declining participation rates are also a challenge for DoD surveys and society more broadly (OPA, 2018e; Miller and Aharoni, 2015; National Research Council, 2013).[15] At the same time, major efforts to combat lower response rates have been increasing, such as using incentives, advance letters, longer fielding periods, additional reminder messages, and mixed survey modes (OPA, 2018e; Miller and Aharoni, 2015; National Research Council, 2013). We consider here a few key factors that could have inhibited participation in the 2017 Air Force Community Feedback Tool.

The survey includes potentially sensitive topics, such as personal problems experienced in the past year, whether respondents contacted a mental health care professional for assistance, and perceived resilience scores. Despite the terms of confidentiality, some individuals may not be comfortable providing this information on an Air Force–sponsored survey. Thus, the survey may err on the side of underreporting rather than overreporting experiences and attitudes that respondents believed could have negative consequences if revealed (regardless of whether they actually would).

---

[15] For example, in 2003 the response rates on the DoD's Status of Forces surveys were 35% for the active component survey and 40% for the reserve component survey. By 2017 those rates had dropped to 20% and 17% respectively, despite an increasing number of reminder messages, survey fielding periods more than doubling and additional efforts to recruit participants (OPA, 2018e).

Some personnel experienced survey access issues. Some individuals who attempted to participate in the survey using their Air Force network computer encountered warning messages or locally blocked access to the .com survey site, despite confirmation from the Secretary of the Air Force's Chief Information Dominance and Chief Information Officer (SAF/CIO A6) that the site was legitimate and verification of the security certificates. Although we and Air Force representatives assisted those who reached out regarding these concerns, it is not likely that everyone who encountered these contacted someone for support. A .com site was used to avoid the access barriers presented by requiring a CAC card for .mil access; however, the lesson from this survey is that technological hurdles may be reduced by providing both .com and .mil pathways to the survey instrument. Furthermore, additional coordination earlier in the process may help, so that SAF/CIO A6 can help remove hurdles at the local or unit level of information security and so that local community support coordinators can assist with testing access prior to survey launch (Air Force users can encounter security certificate warnings or blocks even when visiting other legitimate .mil websites). A telephone option for survey participation would be another way to facilitate access, particularly for personnel willing to participate but facing barriers to web-based participation.

It was more difficult to reach spouses to invite them to the survey because the Air Force personnel files do not include spouse email addresses. The process for requesting and obtaining access to that information from the Defense Manpower Data Center (DMDC) would have extended beyond the Air Force's desired survey time frame. Thus, we mailed postcards for spouses to the homes of married airmen, using first class postage so that it would be forwarded if the family had recently moved. We do not know how the postcard recruitment approach compares with email in terms of trust and appeal, accuracy of the contact information, and success in reaching today's Air Force spouses. However, had both options been feasible, it would have been preferable to use both.

Additionally, despite initial attempts to deconflict spouse survey fielding dates, the fielding of DoD's 2017 Active Duty Spouse Survey (June–November 2017) preceded and overlapped the Air Force's (August–October 2017), and the fielding of the 2017 Reserve Component Spouse Survey (February–July 2017) concluded just prior. Thus, it is possible that some Air Force spouses who were in the DoD sample did not distinguish between the two surveys or did not wish to complete two. Air Force personnel may have also been asked to participate in other surveys during this period.

In Appendix B, we consider the costs and potential benefits of additional strategies that might have been able to increase the response rate (although not necessarily change the overall Air Force results) and offer recommendations for future survey administration. Greater response rates, particularly from some of the smaller segments of the community (e.g., those at the smaller guard installations) would enable fuller reporting of results at the installation level and greater understanding of subgroup variation in the Air Force–level analyses. As noted earlier, higher response rates do not necessarily eliminate the potential for bias. A nonresponse bias study would need to be conducted before conclusions could be drawn.

Analyses and Reporting

This report highlights key results from analyses that were prioritized over other possibilities to address the primary objectives of the 2017 Air Force Community Feedback Tool. It focuses on items that were a top priority for the Air Force (e.g., perceptions of resilience), that point to where the greatest need may be (e.g., those whose mental or physical health was limiting their activities), and that may lead to feasible recommendations for improvement. Thus, this is not an exhaustive report of all analyses of potential value. At the conclusion of this report, we recommend follow-on analyses that may provide additional value to the Air Force.

One strength of this survey is the large number of respondents. Still, regression analyses can support only a limited number of demographic, military service, and installation characteristic variables, particularly for binary and categorical outcomes. Thus, in consultation with the sponsor, we prioritized both which survey items to analyze and which characteristics to include as explanatory variables.

The availability of demographic and military service variables in the Air Force personnel data set varied by subgroup. For example, the Air Force does not track marital status or child status for civilian employees as it does for airmen whose spouses and children are military dependents and beneficiaries of such services as military health care. Also, we cannot identify from the personnel data set which civilian employees are spouses of airmen. Thus, we could not create a weighted sample that would combine the spouse and personnel data sets because doing so would double count employees who are also spouses. Air Force personnel data on spouses are fairly limited, so we did not have information on standard demographic characteristics, such as spouse age, gender, and race or ethnicity.

Our narrative description focuses on results that were both statistically significant and potentially large enough or interpretable enough to be meaningful (i.e., findings that were both statistically and meaningfully different). To streamline presentation, we present only results that met both criteria. This means that, in some cases, overall effects were significant, but individual coefficients were not significant at $p < 0.001$ and, hence, were not described. However, this is partly dependent on our choice of referent category, and we did not examine all possible comparisons. In some cases, overall effects were significant but did not satisfy our criteria for being a key finding. In general, the following characteristics were included for airmen: component (referent category, active component); rank group (referent, junior enlisted); military career group (referent, operations); hours worked per week on Air Force duties (referent, less than 40); nights away from home because of Air Force duties in past year (referent, 0 to 29); distance from base (referent, lives on base); marital status (referent, unmarried and not in a committed romantic relationship); and dependent minor children (referent, no children).[16] Characteristics for Air Force civilians included the following: type of employee (referent, appropriated fund General Schedule employees); whether or not an employee was also an airman; whether or not an employee was a veteran; hours worked per week on Air Force duties (referent, less than 40); distance from base (referent, living on base); marital status (referent unmarried and not in a committed romantic relationship); and has minor children (referent, no children). The following characteristics were included in spouse models: component of their airman (referent, active); rank group of their airman (referent, junior enlisted airman);[17] hours their airman worked per week on Air Force duties (referent, less than 40); distance from base (referent, lives on base); whether or not they themselves were employed at least part time outside the home; and has minor children (referent, no children). Location characteristics (common across airman, civilian, and spouse models) included four dummy variables, with the referent being the absence in each case: located in a foreign country, base not led by the Air Force, remote or isolated location, and location other than at a base (e.g., at a recruiting station).We did not conduct all possible comparisons with all possible referent groups: For example, we compare married airmen with airmen who are unmarried and not in a committed romantic relationship but cannot speak to potential differences between married airmen and those with significant others. Still, for each of our variables, we believe we have captured the major comparisons likely of greatest interest to the Air Force.

As an example of what this means in practice, marital status was significant as a block for choice of work-life balance as a top problem for airmen. However, neither unmarried but partnered airmen nor married airmen were significantly different from the referent category of unmarried, uncommitted airmen. Thus, we do not discuss this finding in the discussion of problem choice models.

Organization of This Report

The body of this report contains selected results from the 2017 Air Force Community Feedback Tool, organized by topic:

---

[16] Further detail on respondent characteristics included may be found in Tables B.5–B.7.

[17] Our unweighted spouse respondents included more than 10% who entered the survey using the Air Force civilian employee survey code emailed to them rather than the spouse code mailed to them, meaning we were unable to link them with their airmen's records. We did not ask Air Force civilian employee respondents married to airmen to provide information on their spouse's rank group, so rather than drop this substantial minority through listwise deletion, we also included a "rank group unknown" comparison group. We compared findings with this "rank group unknown" comparison group against analyses that did not include this group in the model and did observe a few meaningful differences in the results for spouse reporting, of which top problem was their sole or most significant type of past-year problem, which we report in Chapter 3. In other models, the "rank group unknown" group had significant associations with the dependent variable; in many cases, the observable change was only that removing the spouses from the model meant that the association of that group with the dependent variable was no longer significant.

- Chapter 2 addresses self-reported health, social support, and perceived resilience.
- Chapter 3 describes problems experienced in the past year and any perceived needs associated with the top type of problem.
- Chapter 4 explores the help-seeking behaviors of those who perceived needs for their top type of problem, as well as whether those who reached out for assistance believed their needs were met.
- Chapter 5 provides general perceptions from across the Air Force about military resources they may or may not have used to meet any of their needs.
- Chapter 6 covers attitudes toward military service or employment, as well as satisfaction with the respect the Air Force shows family members.
- Chapter 7 explores associations between key indicators of interest on the survey, such as whether there was an association between unmet needs and attitudes toward military service.
- Chapter 8 offers conclusions and recommendations for further analyses and for action, based on some of the key findings from our analyses.

The appendixes provide additional details on survey methods and results:

- Appendix A lists the servicing locations for Air Force personnel and the DRUs and MAJCOMs responsible for these locations.
- Appendix B provides additional methodological details, including more information about the survey framework and content, the survey recruitment and marketing plan, how the results were weighted, and more-detailed recommendations for future survey administration.
- Appendix C contains tables of respondent and location characteristics.
- Appendix D reports frequencies of specific problems experienced in the past year.
- Appendix E contains a detailed summary of health and health-system related information.

2. Self-Rated Health and Resilience-Related Measures

This report focuses on the findings from the 2017 Air Force Community Feedback Tool that are most relevant for community planning: indicators of health and well-being, attitudes toward military service, the problems that Air Force community members face, any needs stemming from these problems, and services used to address these problems. This chapter addresses the following questions:

- How did respondents rate their own general health?
- To what degree did poor health interfere with daily activities?
- What characterized respondents' social support networks?
- How did respondents score themselves on a measure of perceived resilience?

This chapter then explores whether self-reported limited activity and perceived resilience varied by selected location, demographic or military service characteristics.

Health-Related Quality of Life

The Centers for Disease Control and Prevention's Health-Related Quality of Life assessment items measure general physical and mental health, including

- one question assessing self-rated health
- two questions assessing the number of "unhealthy days" a participant has experienced in the past month due to physical or mental problems
- one question asking respondents with any unhealthy days whether poor physical or mental health interfered with usual activities, such as self-care, work, or recreation (Centers for Disease Control and Prevention, 2016).

These four items were included in this survey, and results are presented in Table 2.1.

Self-rated health was assessed through the question, "Would you say that in general your health is excellent, very good, good, fair, or poor?" Overall, 56% of Air Force personnel and 59% of spouses of airmen indicated that their health is excellent or very good. We did not test for significant differences across the descriptive results.[18] However, in examining the results, it is evident that employees appeared to rate their health lower than did airmen and spouses, which was not unexpected. Service members tend to be relatively young and healthy by design, given the physical requirements and stressors of military service, and they become eligible for retirement after 20 years of service. Civilian employees, however, are not similarly screened for

---

[18] Because of the large number of respondents, significance tests between these major subgroups would tend to show statistically significant differences that could be based on sample size alone and that would not have meaningful or practical value for the Air Force (e.g., where there is only a 1-percentage-point difference between groups). Thus, testing for statistical significance across the descriptive analyses was not a priority relative to other opportunities for analysis.

physical health conditions and include personnel with disabilities that would disqualify individuals from military service. Employees (with five years of service) are eligible for retirement much later, at age 62. Thus, the average age of airmen is 28 for the enlisted force and 35 for officers, while the average age for civilian employees is 48 (Air Force Personnel Center, 2018a).

Table 2.1. Health-Related Quality-of-Life Indicators, by Subgroup

	Active	Guard	Reserve	Employee	Personnel Overall	Spouses of Airmen
Self-rated health (%)						
Excellent	21	22	27	12	20	18
Very good	36	39	38	32	36	41
Good	33	32	29	40	34	32
Fair	9	7	5	14	9	7
Poor	1	1	1	2	1	1
Past month unhealthy days (average number)						
Physical	4.2	3.0	2.8	4.2	3.9	3.3
Mental	3.7	2.4	2.2	3.7	3.4	4.5
Limited-activity days (average number)						
Those with 1–30	4.9	3.5	3.6	3.9	4.3	3.5
Those with 0–30	2.9	1.8	1.7	2.6	2.5	2.5
Ns	20,958–34,783	4,543–8,752	2,103–4,343	15,508–23,491	42,143–70,009	4,344–6,222

NOTES: This self-rated health measure is part of the Health-Related Quality of Life assessment (Centers for Disease Control and Prevention, 2016). Responses from individuals who are both airmen and employees are included in both subgroups' results. Responses from civilian employees who are also spouses of airmen are included in both subgroups' results. Shading across the self-rated health rows highlights the most common response for each subgroup of respondents.

Table 2.1 also displays the average number of self-reported "unhealthy days" experienced in the month prior to the survey. The question on physical health asked: "Now thinking about your physical health, which includes physical illness and injury, how many days during the past 30 days was your physical health not good?" The mental health variation asked this: "Now thinking about your mental health, which includes stress, depression, and problems with emotions, how many days during the past 30 days was your mental health not good?" On average, the number of self-reported poor physical health days in the past month was 3.9 among Air Force personnel and 3.3 among spouses of airmen. The average number of self-reported poor mental health days in the past month was 3.4 among Air Force personnel and 4.5 among spouses of airmen.[19] Note that

---

[19] As a reference, among American adults ages 18–44, the average number of self-reported poor physical health days in the past month was 2.6 (United Health Foundation, 2018a), and the average number of self-reported poor

these days are not necessarily additive: An individual could have a day on which they were unhealthy both physically and mentally.

Air Force community members who reported any unhealthy days in the past month were asked a follow-up question: "During the past 30 days, approximately how many days did poor physical or mental health keep you from doing your usual activities, such as self-care, work, or recreation?" The item provides no further definition, so limited activity could range from individuals who were generally functioning but forgoing routine workouts to individuals who were unable to get out of bed. Among those with any unhealthy days in the past 30 days, 53% of Air Force personnel and 53% of spouses reported having one or more days on which their health kept them from their usual activities. Focusing on only the respondents who had any self-reported days in the past month that poor health kept them from their usual activities, the average number of unhealthy days was 4.3 for Air Force personnel and 3.5 for spouses of airmen. When we also include respondents who experienced *no* unhealthy days in the past month to calculate the average number of limited-activity days across the entire population, the average number of self-reported days that poor health kept anyone from their usual activities was 2.5 for Air Force personnel and 2.5 for spouses of airmen.

Social Support Networks

Certain aspects of military life, such as permanent change of station moves, can disrupt social support networks, but other aspects, such as shared values and experiences, may enhance them. Social support networks can be important sources of emotional or social support, a sense of belonging, resources and services (e.g., loans, rides, babysitting), and advice or information (e.g., resources available, job opportunities). People whose personal networks do not have the ability or resources to help them may depend more heavily on programs and services for assistance or may go without help.

Survey participants were asked to indicate whether certain statements apply to their personal networks of friends and family. Figure 2.1 shows the characteristics of Air Force personnel's social support networks across four dimensions (Miller et al., 2011), worded as the items appeared in the survey. Overall, 90% or more in each subgroup felt there is at least one person they can always count on to "be there" for them; however, about 50% of respondents said they do not like to reveal their problems or needs to their friends and family. Compared with the more geographically stable guard and reserve airmen and civilian employees, a larger percentage of active component airmen felt that most or all of their friends and family live too far away from

---

mental health days was 4.2 (United Health Foundation, 2018b). We caution against drawing conclusions based on comparisons with the Air Force results, however, because differences may be due to differences in survey methods or demographic characteristics (e.g., gender ratio).

them. In addition, overall, 21% of Air Force personnel combined (not shown the figure) reported that the people in their personal networks do not have the ability or resources to help them.

Figure 2.1. Air Force Personnel's Agreement That Each Characteristic Describes Their Social Support Networks, by Subgroup

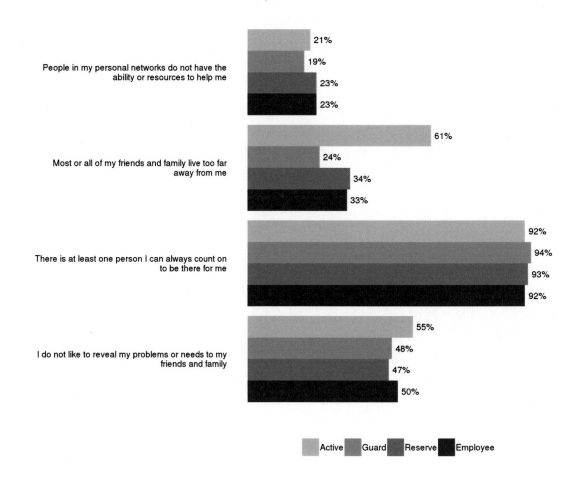

NOTES: *N* = 41,286 active, 10,019 guard, 5,063 reserve, and 27,067 employees. Responses from individuals who are in more than one subgroup are included in each subgroups' results.

Spouses' ratings of their social support networks, shown in Figure 2.2, were similar to those shown in Figure 2.1. Most (91%) felt that there is at least one person they can count on; however, about one of every ten spouses did not feel that way. As with personnel, 21% of spouses believed the people in their personal networks do not have the ability or resources to help them.

Figure 2.2. Spouses' Agreement That Each Characteristic Describes Their Social Support Networks

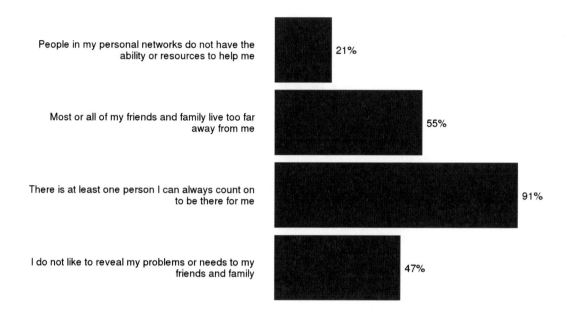

NOTE: *N* = 6,224 spouses.

Perceived Resilience

The Air Force adopted a broad definition of *resilience* that generally aligns with the psychological literature's use of the term and that was put forth by both the Institute of Medicine and the Defense Centers of Excellence for Psychological Health and Traumatic Brain Injury: "The ability to withstand, recover, and grow in the face of stressors and changing demands" (AFI 90-506, 2014; Meadows, Miller, and Robson, 2015; Meadows et al., 2015).

The Air Force requested that the 2017 Air Force Community Feedback Tool include the short-form version of the previously developed Connor-Davidson Resilience Scale (CD-RISC 10), which contains ten questions about perceptions of resiliency during the past month (Connor and Davidson, 2003). The Air Force had used this proprietary scale in the 2013 Community Assessment Survey (the predecessor to the current survey) and obtained a license to use it again in 2017. The questions in the scale relate to various topics, including asking respondents whether they are able to adapt to change, can deal with whatever comes, and see the humorous side of things (Connor and Davidson, 2003). With this measure, respondents are not given examples of context to consider (e.g., how they believed they would respond to particular situations, such as a move, serious injury, death of a loved one) but are instead asked to reflect on their own resilience in general terms. These items were developed to function as a scale (i.e., measuring a construct together as a group) rather than as individual items.[20] Respondents are asked to indicate on a 5-point scale (scored from 0 to 4 points) how often these statements are true for them. Summing responses across all ten items, possible scores range from 0 (lowest) to 40 (highest). In this survey, Air Force personnel had an average perceived resilience score of 31.8; for spouses, the average score was 29.6. Table 2.2 shows these average scores by subgroup.

Table 2.2. Average Perceived Resilience Total Score Out of a Possible Score of 40, by Subgroup

	Active	Guard	Reserve	Employee	Personnel Overall	Spouses of Airmen
Air Force	31.2	32.4	32.9	31.9	31.8	29.6
Ns	35,590	8,960	4,496	23,950	71,598	6,786

NOTE: This represents respondents' general perceptions of their own resilience and does not necessarily predict how resilient individuals might be in various situations. Responses from individuals who are both airmen and employees are included in both subgroups' results. Responses from civilian employees who are also spouses of airmen are included in both subgroups' results.

In the 2013 Air Force Community Assessment survey, the average perceived resilience score (CD-RISC 10) for airmen was 32.4 (standard deviation [SD] 6.11) (Dixon, 2016, p. 94). In the study used to first develop the ten-item version of the scale, the average score from a U.S. national random digit dial sample was 32.1 (Connor and Davidson, 2003). A subsequent community telephone survey of adults in randomly sampled households from metropolitan Memphis, Tennessee, found an average score of 31.8 (Campbell-Sills, Forde, and Stein, 2009). A small study of U.S. Army couples in which one or both individuals had deployed to military operations in Iraq or Afghanistan found low variability in CD-RISC 10 scores, with a mean of 31.0 (SD 6.5) (Melvin et al., 2012, p. 174). In the current survey, the average score among airmen was 31.8 (SD 6.5), and the scale had an alpha of 0.93. Thus, in terms of the overall averages, there is little to remark on, other than the apparent relative consistency of scores using this particular scale.

Previous studies of U.S. populations that used this resilience measure found that individuals with posttraumatic stress disorder or exposure to severe trauma had average scores of 28.5 (SD 5.5; Grattan et al., 2011), 29.9 (SD 6.3; McCanlies et al., 2014), 31.0 (SD 6.5; Melvin et al., 2012), and 31.3 (SD 6.6; Rainey et al., 2014). However, there is no standard set of discrete cutoff scores that distinguishes vulnerable from resilient populations, so we cannot draw conclusions regarding any seeming similarity or difference in scores.

---

[20] Because these items are proprietary, we cannot publish the individual items. A list of abbreviated items from the 25-item version of the CD-RISC is published in Table 1 of Bezdjian et al., 2017. Further information about the scale and terms of use can be found on the CD-RISC website.

Exploring Variation in Responses: Limited-Activity Days and Perceived Resilience

As noted in our analytic approach, as described in Chapter 1, we used statistical models to explore whether the responses to a subset of items varied by certain location or individual characteristics, and we ran separate models for airmen, civilian employees, and spouses of airmen.[21] Within the general domain of self-rated health and resilience-related measures, we focused on two items for further exploration:

- **Limited-activity days.** This item was selected because of its focus on physical or mental health issues that reached the level of disrupting daily activities, thereby filtering out minor issues. This number included those who indicated that they had not had any poor health days in the previous month, who would otherwise have not been asked the question. They were coded as "0." In reviewing our regression results, we focused on identifying differences between groups that represented approximately one fewer day or more of limited activity in the past month.

- **Perceived resilience.** This scale was selected because the Air Force (and DoD more broadly) has developed policies and programs aimed at fostering resilience (Air Force Instruction 90-506, 2014; Air Force Instruction 90-506, 2014). Past Air Force surveys have used either the ten- or 25-item version of this proprietary measure (Bezdjian et al., 2017; Dixon, 2016). Previous reports suggested that the single-factor, ten-item version of the CD-RISC might not be the best fit for the airman population (Bezdjian et al., 2017; Dixon, 2016; Dixon and Bares, 2018). We explore whether there was any significant and noteworthy variation in airmen, employee, and spouse perceptions of their own resilience. Given that the scale scores range from 0 to 40, we focused on statistically significant differences in scores of 2 points or more on this scale. Although these differences were relatively small, we wanted to highlight for Air Force leadership where we found the largest differences. Again our aim was to bring to the fore the characteristics associated with the greatest magnitude of statistically significant differences.

Inclusion of the selected location, demographic, and service history characteristics was guided by both practical and theoretical considerations as well as Air Force priorities. The goal was to cover key characteristics that could be helpful to Air Force CABs and Community Action Teams in targeting interventions within the community.[22] As described in Chapter 1, we also included a set of variables describing problem-solving status but, in this case, only for limited-activity days because the resilience items also address how one responds to challenges.

For the domain of health and resilience, it is possible that reported differences might be associated with factors related to status and access to resources available from the military, as found in prior research (Brown et al., 2015; Meadows et al., 2018; Sims et al., 2017; Sims et al., 2018). For example, working particularly long hours on a persistent basis may negatively affect

---

[21] For technical readers, output with full model results is available from the authors.

[22] The Community Action Team was formerly known as the Integrated Delivery System.

physical or mental health, and opportunities for self-care or to seek health care may be limited. Spouses whose airmen were frequently deployed or otherwise serving away from home and thus have often had to manage the household alone may have perceived themselves as more or less resilient than other spouses, depending on how well they have been able to manage.

We explored the potential relevance of base location, for multiple reasons. First, for outreach and program planning purposes, Air Force leaders may wish to know whether community members at certain types of locations feel more limited by their health or less resilient. Patterns may suggest where additional support is needed. The location itself could play a role. For example, individuals living in a foreign country could struggle with adapting to a different culture, functioning in an area where English is not always used, or connecting to friends and family who live far away and in vastly different time zones. These experiences could take a toll on an individual's well-being and their own assessment of how well they handle life's difficulties. Military policies attempt to mitigate some of the challenges of being assigned to installations in remote and isolated location through additional levels of appropriated funds to support morale, welfare, and recreation (e.g., AFI 65-106, 2009).

Thus, in general, we employed the location, demographic, and military service characteristics listed in Table 1.3 in our airman, spouse, and civilian employee models for limited-activity days due to poor health and members' perceptions of their own resilience. We found that location differences did not meet our criteria for statistical significance described earlier. A few military service or demographic characteristics stood out because of their associations with reported limited-activity days or perceived resilience.

Airmen

Controlling for the other characteristics in the models, the following characteristics were associated with airmen reporting about 1 *less* day in the past month on which usual activities, such as self-care, work, or recreation, were limited by poor physical or mental health:

- typically working less than 40 hours a week performing Air Force duties (compared with typically working 50 or more hours a week)
- living on base (compared with living 30 minutes or more away from base)
- being in the guard or reserve, compared with being in the active component
- being a senior officer, compared with being a junior enlisted airman.

Additionally, compared with airmen whose needs for their greatest past-year problem went unmet despite reaching out for help, airmen with the following problem-solving statuses were associated with reporting *fewer* limited-activity days in the past month:

- Not having problems in the past year was associated with almost 4 fewer limited-activity days in the past month.
- Not needing help for the top past-year problem or having a need but then not reaching out for assistance because the problem was otherwise solved was associated with 2.5 and 2.8 fewer days, respectively.

- Having a need but not reaching out for some other reason (i.e., belief there is nothing anyone can do, did not want to ask for help, or did not know who to contact) was associated with about 2 fewer days.
- Being able to successfully meet one's needs for the top past-year problem after reaching out for assistance was also associated with about 2 fewer days in the past month that were limited due to poor physical or mental health.

Few characteristics were related to airmen's perceptions of their own resilience. Controlling for all other characteristics,

- Reserve airmen's average perceived resilience scores were 2 points *higher* than active component airmen's average scores.
- Senior officers' average scores were 2 points *higher* than junior enlisted airmen's.

Any other differences that may be associated with the characteristics in Table 2.3 reflected less than a 2-point difference between average perceived resilience scores, on a 40-point scale.

Table 2.3. Overview of Characteristics Associated with Notable Differences in Airmen's Self-Reported Limited-Activity Days Due to Poor Health and Perceived Resilience Scores

		Limited-Activity Days	Perceived Resilience
Location	U.S. or foreign		
	Remote and isolated		
	Non–Air Force–led installation		
	Somewhere other than an installation		
Military service	Component	✓	✓
	Rank group	✓	✓
	Military career group		
	Distance from base	✓	
	Personnel nights away from home		
	Personnel hours working Air Force duties	✓	
Demographic	Marital status		
	Minor child(ren)		
Problem-solving status[a]		✓	—

NOTES: These regression model results show statistically significant differences ($p < 0.001$) of at least one limited-activity day or a 2-point difference in perceived resilience scores, controlling for all other included location and individual demographic and military service characteristics.

[a]Not included in resilience model.

Spouses of Airmen

Controlling for all other characteristics, the following were associated with spouses of airmen reporting about 1 *less* day in the past month where usual activities, such as self-care, work, or recreation, were limited by poor physical or mental health:

- being married to either a junior or senior officer (compared with being married to an airman who is junior enlisted)
- having a minor child or children
- being employed or self-employed.

Problem-solving status was also relevant for spouses.[23] Compared with spouses who had unmet needs for their top past-year problem despite contacting someone for assistance,

- Not having problems in the past year was associated with about 3 fewer limited-activity days in the past month, as was having a need but skipping follow-up questions about whether any resources were contacted.
- Not needing help for the top past-year problem was associated with about 2 fewer limited-activity days.
- Perceiving a need associated with the top problem but not reaching out for help for some reason other than the problem being resolved was associated with about 1 less day.
- Successfully meeting one's needs after reaching out for help was associated with about 1.5 fewer days in the past month where activities were limited because of poor health.

Few characteristics were related to spouse's perceptions of their own resilience. Controlling for all other characteristics, being married to a senior officer was associated with a 2.5-point higher perceived resilience score than being married to a junior enlisted airman. Spouses for whom their airman's rank was unknown also tended to have higher scores than spouses known to be married to junior enlisted airmen, by about 3.5 points. However, these ranks were unknown because these spouses were also civilian employees, and the survey asked about their own employee status rather than their airman's rank. This suggests that, compared with spouses of junior enlisted airmen, spouses with their own attachment to the Air Force through their employment perceived themselves as more resilient. Any other differences associated with the characteristics in Table 1.3 reflected a difference of less than 2 points between average perceived resilience scores among spouses of airmen who are not airmen themselves.

---

[23] For spouses, the status of having needs associated with a sole or most significant past-year problem, but not reaching out for help and not indicating why on the survey, dropped out of the model because very few spouses fit this category.

Table 2.4. Overview of Characteristics Associated with Notable Differences in Spouse Self-Reported Limited-Activity Days Due to Poor Health and Perceived Resilience Scores

		Limited-Activity Days	Perceived Resilience
Location	U.S. or foreign		
	Remote and isolated		
	Non–Air Force–led installation		
	Somewhere other than an installation		
Military service[a]	Component		
	Rank group[b]	✓	✓
	Distance from base		
	Personnel nights away from home		
	Personnel hours working Air Force duties		
Demographic	Spouse employment	✓	✓
	Minor child(ren)	✓	
Problem-solving status[c]		✓	—

NOTES: These regression model results show statistically significant differences ($p < 0.001$) of at least one limited-activity day or 2-point difference in perceived resilience scores, controlling for all other included location and individuals' demographic and military service characteristics.
[a] In the spouse models, component, rank group, nights away from home and hours working refer to their airmen's characteristics.
[b] Not asked of spouses who are also civilian employees.
[c] Not included in resilience model.

Civilian Employees

Among Air Force civilian employees, relatively few characteristics were associated with a statistically significant difference of 1 day or more in the number of days in the past month on which usual activities, such as self-care, work, or recreation, were limited by poor physical or mental health. Controlling for all other characteristics, problem-solving status was the only characteristic that met our dual criteria. Compared with Air Force civilians who had unmet needs for their greatest past-year problem despite contacting someone for assistance,

- Not having problems in the past year was associated with almost 4 fewer limited-activity days in the past month.
- Having a need for the top past-year problem but not reaching out for help and not indicating why was associated with about 3 fewer days.
- Not perceiving a need for help with the top past-year problem or perceiving a need for help with the top problem but not reaching out because the problem was otherwise solved was associated with between 2.5 and 3 fewer limited-activity days.
- Not reaching out for help for some other reason (other than it being solved) or successfully meeting one's needs after reaching out were both associated with about 1.5 fewer past month limited-activity days that were due to poor health.

Thus, compared with most of their counterparts, the civilian employees who reached out for help with their top past-year problem but whose needs were still unmet were likely to have more days in the past month where their personal or professional activities were limited by poor physical or mental health.

Air Force civilian employee's perceptions of their own resilience were relatively consistent, with no characteristics rising to the level of being statistically significant and representing at least a 2-point difference on a 40-point scale in average ratings between subgroups.

Findings and Conclusions

More than 55% of community members believed that their health was excellent or very good, and only 1 to 2% rated it as poor. Still, across the population, members reported that there were about two to three days in the past month on which poor mental or physical health kept them from their usual activities, such as self-care, work, or recreation. Fortunately, 90% or more of community members in each subgroup felt there was at least one person they could always count on to "be there" for them. About 50% of respondents said they do not like to reveal their problems or needs to their friends and family, so they may have a limited network they feel comfortable to draw on for help. Moreover, about 20% of community members reported that their personal networks do not have the resources or ability to help them. Turning to the measure of perceived resilience, scores within the Air Force community were similar to those in the general population and varied very little across subgroups of airmen, civilian employees, and spouses.

Within the general domain of self-rated health and resilience-related measures, we focused on two items for further exploration: limited days (because of its focus on physical or mental health issues that reached the level of disrupting daily activities, thereby filtering out minor issues) and resilience (because both the Air Force and DoD focus more broadly on interventions aimed at improving resilience). Factors associated with availability of resources, such as higher ranks for airmen and their spouses and spouse employment, tended to be related both to fewer days on which activities were limited by poor health and higher ratings of their own resilience. Given the definitional and temporal ambiguity associated with the rather general resilience construct itself (similar to the challenge of the general concepts of "well-being" or "health"), developing specific, robust interventions or targets for intervention is likely to prove difficult based on a scale score. In the airmen, spouse, and employee models, those who reached out for assistance with their top past-year problem but did not end up getting the help they needed tended to fare worse than their counterparts. As one might expect, those who reported having confronted no problems in the past year, or having problems but no corresponding need for assistance with their top problem, had among the fewest days in the past month where they felt limited by their health. Among airmen and civilian employees, not having problems in the past year was associated with almost 4 fewer limited-activity days in the past month, and among spouses of airmen, it was associated with more than 3 fewer limited-activity days. In some senses, this is similar to the phenomenon when individuals seek mental health care. Care may improve their outcomes and is essential to provide for this reason. But simply not having a mental health challenge at all, or facing a relatively minor challenge, is a better outcome still.

3. Self-Reported Problems and Needs in the Past Year

The 2017 Air Force Community Feedback Tool asked respondents to indicate the problems they faced in the past year, then followed up with those who had problems to learn how they prioritized their problems (if they had more than one type); what their perceived needs were for their sole or most significant type of problem, if they sought help to meet these needs; and how perceived needs related to their top type of problem. We then explored what demographic and military service characteristics were associated with the problems for the Air Force community.

Types of Problems: All and Sole or Most Significant

This section answers the following questions:

- How many Air Force personnel faced problems in the 12 months prior to the survey?
- What types of problems did they face?
- What were the top problems they faced?
- How intense did the problems become?

Survey participants were asked to indicate, from across a wide range of problems, which ones they had experienced in the previous 12 months. Table 3.1 provides examples of specific problems within the problem types included in the survey. Appendix B includes a complete list of possible problems presented on the survey, with notes indicating where items were worded differently or displayed only for different demographic subgroups (e.g., guard members, employees).

Who Faced No Problems?

Notably, 10% of Air Force personnel reported no problems in the past year in any of the problem types. By subgroup, the following indicated that they had faced none of the types of problems described in Table 3.1:

- 7% of active component
- 15% of guard
- 13% of reserve
- 12% of civilian employees.

Among Air Force spouses, 8% reported experiencing no problems in the past year.

Table 3.1. Problem Types, with Examples of Specific Issues

Types of Problems	Example Issues Respondents May Select
Military practices and culture	• Adjusting to military language, organization, culture • Lack of support for your professional/career development • Poor relationship with coworkers or superiors
Work-life balance	• Finding time for enough sleep, a healthy diet, or physical exercise • Work hours, schedule, or commute to work
Household management	• Moving or storage of belongings • Theft, break-in, or vandalism of home or property
Financial or legal	• Trouble budgeting, paying debt or bills • Child custody, divorce, or other family legal problems
Health care system	• Poor military health care for ongoing/long-term injuries or illnesses • Getting a timely appointment at a military treatment facility • Getting permission to go to a medical appointment during duty hours
Romantic relationships	• Trouble starting a relationship • Divorce/marital separation/end of relationship • Changing roles or responsibilities in the family/marriage
Child specific (asked only of those with minor children)	• Availability of quality youth and teen programs (waiting list, hours, priorities, etc.) • Child's poor or dropping grades • Child's emotional or behavior problems
Own well-being	• Pain, physical injury, or illness • Hard to focus, concentrate, or remember things • Difficulty finding meaning or purpose in life
Spouse or romantic partner's problems (asked only of those with spouses or partners/significant others)	• Physical health • Work or school-related problems • Substance misuse or abuse (alcohol, tobacco, drugs)
Other problems	• Respondents were able to write in up to three specific problems not previously listed

What Types of Problems Did Air Force Community Members Face?

Table 3.2 offers a snapshot of how many Air Force personnel experienced the types of problems shown in Table 3.1. To clarify how these statistics were calculated, the Air Force personnel results for the child-specific problem type should be read as the percentage of Air Force personnel in the community who were managing child-related problems in the past year, not the percentage of Air Force personnel with children who were managing them. Blue shading highlights the three most commonly selected problem types, which in all cases were military practices and culture, work-life balance, and the respondent's own well-being, although not all were endorsed in the same order across subpopulations.

31

**Table 3.2. Types of Problems the Air Force Community Faced Over
the Previous 12 Months, by Air Force Status (%)**

	Active	Guard	Reserve	Employee	Personnel Overall	Spouses of Airmen
Military practices and culture	65	50	56	59	60	53
Work-life balance	67	56	58	52	60	63
Household management	46	37	39	35	41	48
Financial or legal	36	36	45	28	35	42
Health care system	46	25	29	30	37	38
Romantic relationships	47	34	35	28	39	43
Child specific	24	20	21	15	21	39
Own well-being	71	56	54	65	65	73
Spouse or romantic partner's problems	35	28	27	31	32	39
Other problems	10	8	10	11	10	16
No problems	7	15	13	12	10	8
*N*s	41,286	10,019	5,063	27,067	81,833	7,434

NOTES: *N*s reflect the number of respondents in each subgroup who either indicated that they had one or more type of problem in the past year or affirmed that they had none. Responses from individuals who are both airmen and employees are included in both subgroups' results. Responses from civilian employees who are also spouses of airmen are included in both subgroups' results. Blue shading highlights the three most commonly selected problem types.

What Types of Problems Were the Sole or Most Significant?

Any respondent who indicated problems in more than one problem type was asked to prioritize the type of problem from the past year that was most significant to them, that is, their top problem. Follow-up questions pertained to the top problem. Those who indicated a problem in only one problem type were asked about that type of problem—because it was the sole problem type reported. In our analyses, we combined the follow-up question responses from participants, regardless of whether they had only one type of problem or had prioritized a problem from among more than one that they experienced. The next figures provide an overview of these combined, top problem types for Air Force personnel (Figure 3.1) and Air Force spouses (Figure 3.2).

For Air Force personnel, note the fairly large gap between the three most common top problems (each experienced by 18–27% of personnel) and the remaining types of problems (each experienced by 3–7% of personnel). Indeed, for 65% of personnel who faced any problems in the past year, the top problem type was military practices and culture, work-life balance, or their own well-being. Among spouses of airmen, the same three types of top problems were most commonly selected, but by 49% of spouses with any problems.

Figure 3.1. Air Force Personnel's Top Type of Problem in the Past Year, Among Those with Any Problems

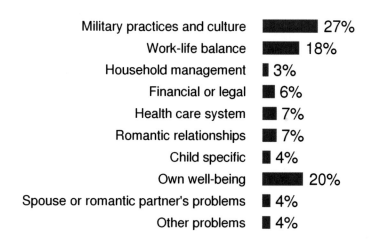

NOTE: *N* = 71,247 personnel. *Top* refers to the sole type of problem experienced in the past year or to the type the respondent prioritized as most significant.

Figure 3.2. Air Force Spouses' Top Type of Problem in the Past Year, Among Those with Any Problems

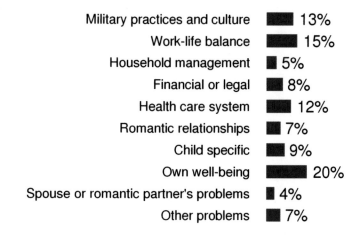

NOTE: *N* = 6,708 spouses. *Top* refers to the sole type of problem experienced in the past year or to the type the respondent prioritized as most significant.

The findings represented in Figures 3.1 and 3.2 differ from Table 3.2 in that they exclude respondents who (a) had no problems or (b) had multiple types of problems but skipped the question asking them to prioritize their problems. For individuals who had any problems, these two figures focus on the sole or the self-reported most significant problem types and omit lower-priority problem types. Common to both the full range of types of problems experienced (Table 3.2) and the top problem types (Figures 3.1. and 3.2), Air Force personnel and spouses of airmen most frequently selected the military practices and culture, own well-being, and work-life balance types.

Appendix D provides additional detail about how many Air Force personnel and spouses experienced specific, more-detailed issues listed within the three most common top problem types. For example, 59% of Air Force personnel who selected military practices and culture as their top type of past-year problem indicated that one of those issues was poor leadership by the military chain of command. Sleeping problems, fatigue, and stress were each reported by about 50% of personnel who selected their own well-being as their top type of past-year problem. Relatedly, among personnel for whom work-life balance was their top type of problem, the most common problems were finding time for enough sleep, a healthy diet or physical exercise (62%); finding time for recreation, stress relief, or family time (59%); and managing many competing commitments, such as work, school, and childcare (57%).

Among spouses who selected their own well-being as their top type of past-year problem, the most frequently reported issues were stress (61%), fatigue (51%), managing weight (50%), and mood (e.g., depression, anger) (48%). Among spouses for whom work-life balance was their top type of problem, the most commonly reported issues were finding enough time for recreation, stress relief, or family time (62%); finding time for enough sleep, a healthy diet or physical exercise (62%); and many competing commitments, such work, school and childcare (60%). Among spouses who selected military practices and culture as their top type of past-year problem, the most commonly selected issue was getting accurate information about when their airmen will have to move, deploy, or travel for work (46%). See Appendix D for further information on other specific issues within the top three problem types.

These problems span both chain of command issues (e.g., perceptions of poor leadership) and issues typically addressed by health care professionals and other service providers (e.g., sleep, stress, mood).

How Intense Did the Top Problems Become?

Air Force planning may benefit from understanding community members' perceived level of severity of their top type of problem, to avoid overinflating issues that might have been common but were experienced as relatively mild. The survey asked respondents who experienced any problems to think about their top type of problem during the past 12 months and indicate how intense that problem was at its worst, with response options of very mild, mild, moderate, and severe. Figure 3.3 shows severity for the top problems for Air Force personnel as a whole. Among personnel who indicated that their top past-year problem type was military practices and culture, romantic relationships, problems their spouse or romantic partner faced, or other types of problems, more than 30% in each category indicated that, at its worst, that type of problem was experienced as severe.

Figure 3.3. Air Force Personnel's Ratings of the Intensity of Their Top Type of Problem in the Past Year (%)

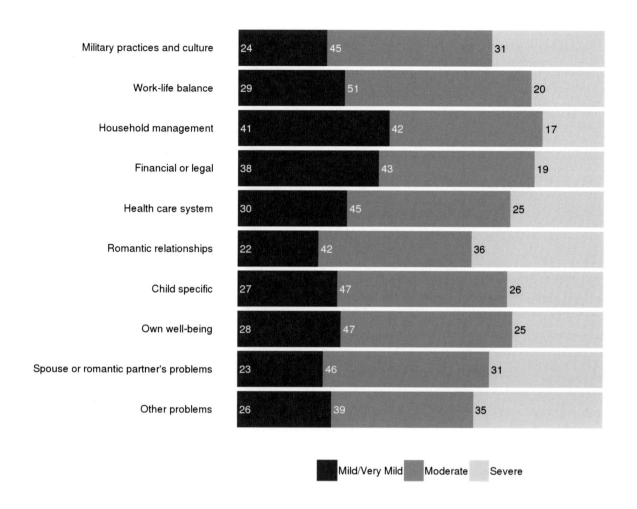

NOTE: *N* = 71,247 personnel. *Top* refers to the sole type of problem experienced in the past year or to the type the respondent prioritized as most significant.

On the other end of the spectrum, 41% of personnel who indicated that household management problems were their top type of problem in the past year rated them as mild or very mild at their worst, and the same was true for 38% of those who selected financial or legal problems as their sole or most significant ones.

Figure 3.4 shows Air Force spouses' severity ratings for their top type of problems experienced in the past year: 45% who experienced romantic relationship problems said that, at their worst, they were severe, while only 15% characterized them as mild or very mild. This was the problem type most commonly rated as severe at its worst.

Figure 3.4. Air Force Spouses' Ratings of the Intensity of Their Top Type of Problem in the Past Year (%)

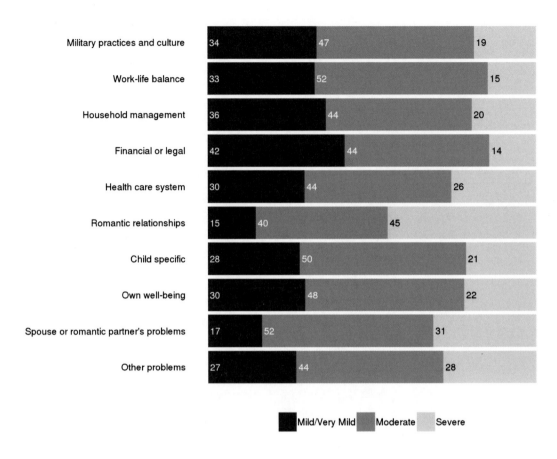

NOTE: *N* = 6,708 spouses. *Top* refers to the sole type of problem experienced in the past year or to the type the respondent prioritized as most significant.

Needs for Assistance with Top Problems

The 2017 Air Force Community Feedback Tool was designed to focus not just on an inventory of problems community members experienced in the past year but also on whether these problems resulted in any needs for assistance. This approach helps Air Force leadership focus its efforts toward the greatest needs, not just the most commonly occurring problems. Thus, this section answers the following questions:

- What needs for assistance resulted from the top problems this population was facing?
- How did needs relate to problem types?
- How did types of needs vary by subgroup?

Survey participants who experienced any problems in the past year were asked to indicate what kinds of help they or their families needed to deal with the type of problem they had prioritized as most significant or as their only type of problem. By *problem type*, we are referring to broader categories, such as "work-life balance" or "romantic relationship problems," not to specific issues within these types of problems. Respondents could choose from the following list of needs, worded here as it appeared on the survey, and could also write in other types of needs:

- general information: for example, about rules or policies or about what is available and how to access it
- specific information: for example, forms, names, dates, step-by-step directions
- an advocate: someone to try to get help for you
- advice, education or coaching: people with experience to recommend the best solution for someone in your situation
- emotional or social support
- professional counseling
- a helping hand: loans, donations, services to help out with some of your responsibilities
- activities or facilities: fitness, recreation, stress relief, family bonding.

Respondents could check all of the needs that applied to their top problem type.

How Many Air Force Community Members Indicated That Their Top Type of Problem Resulted in Needs for Assistance?

Among the Air Force personnel who experienced problems in the past year, 40% reported not needing assistance for their top type of problem.

By subgroup, the following indicated that they had experienced a problem but reported no need for assistance:

- 36% of active component
- 45% of guard
- 41% of reserve
- 46% of civilian employees.

The survey asked these participants to report the main reason they or their families had no need for assistance with their top type of problem. Among this subset of 27,340 Air Force personnel,

- 20% already solved the problem by themselves
- 30% were in the process of solving the problem themselves
- 2% indicated that the problem went away on its own
- 6% expected the problem to go away on its own
- 23% believed there was nothing anyone could do to help solve the problem
- 18% indicated that there was some other reason they had no need for assistance.

Among Air Force spouses, 33% experienced problems but reported not needing assistance. Among this subset of 2,186 spouses,

- 22% already solved the problem by themselves
- 32% were in the process of solving the problem themselves
- 2% indicated that the problem went away on its own
- 6% expected the problem to go away on its own

- 22% believed there was nothing anyone could do to help solve the problem
- 16% indicated that there was some other reason they had no need for assistance.

What Perceived Needs Stemmed from the Top Types of Problem in the Past Year?

It is important to consider the perceived needs and types of help community members might be seeking for their problems because these might not always align with the types of help that Air Force professionals are offering, who is providing it, or how that help is characterized (e.g., as counseling rather than coaching). Figure 3.5 reflects the responses from Air Force personnel who had problems, regarding all the needs they reported having for their top problem.

Figure 3.5. Among Air Force Personnel with Problems and Needs in the Past Year, All Self-Reported Needs for Their Top Type of Problem

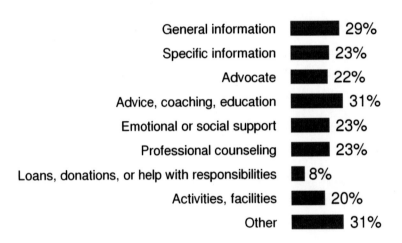

NOTE: *N* = 42,257 personnel. *Top* refers to the sole type of problem experienced in the past year or to the type the respondent prioritized as most significant.

Although a formal content analysis of written comments was beyond the scope of this effort, examples from the "other" category here include those related to a need for improved leadership or culture (e.g., a need for competent leaders or supervisors, leaders who will hold people accountable for not doing their job or inappropriate behavior) or a need for improved availability or quality of medical services (e.g., competent doctors, more referrals, timely appointments, greater Tricare coverage).

Figure 3.6 shows spouses' perceived needs for their top type of problem.

Figure 3.6. Among Spouses with Problems and Needs in the Past Year, All Self-Reported Needs for Their Top Type of Problem

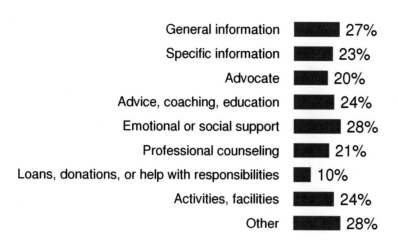

General information 27%
Specific information 23%
Advocate 20%
Advice, coaching, education 24%
Emotional or social support 28%
Professional counseling 21%
Loans, donations, or help with responsibilities 10%
Activities, facilities 24%
Other 28%

NOTE: *N* = 4,445 spouses. *Top* refers to the sole type of problem experienced in the past year or to the type the respondent prioritized as most significant.

Figures 3.5 and 3.6 described **all self-reported needs** associated with three problem types personnel most commonly indicated was their sole or most significant ones. The survey asked those who had more than two needs for their problem to prioritize their two greatest needs. Specifically, the survey software displayed a list of the needs they had already selected, and asked respondents to "please pick which TWO you think were the greatest, most significant needs you had." Thus, we also report on the **two greatest needs that respondents selected**, regardless of their top type of problem. Figure 3.7 displays the two needs prioritized as greatest by Air Force personnel who experienced a problem in the past year, and Figure 3.8 displays that same type of information for spouses of airmen.

Figure 3.7. Greatest Self-Reported Needs for Top Problem Types, Among Air Force Personnel Who Experienced a Problem in the Past Year

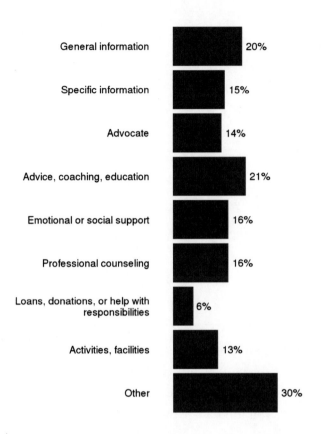

NOTE: *N* = 42,225 personnel. *Top* refers to the sole type of problem experienced in the past year or to the type the respondent prioritized as most significant.

Figure 3.8. Greatest Self-Reported Needs for Top Problem Types, Among Spouses Who Experienced a Problem in the Past Year

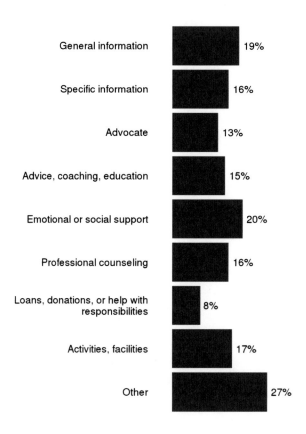

NOTE: *N* = 4,445 spouses. *Top* refers to the sole type of problem experienced in the past year or to the type the respondent prioritized as most significant.

How Did Needs Relate to Top Problem Type?

Table 3.3 shows how Air Force personnel's two greatest needs map onto their top problem, for the subset of personnel whose top problem was among the three most common across the Air Force. The percentages represent how many personnel, out of those who had a problem in the past year, indicated that a given need resulted from a given type of problem. Individuals may be represented in two cells because they were able to select the two needs they thought applied to their particular top problem type.

Table 3.3. Two Greatest Self-Reported Needs for the Top Three Types of Problems, Among Air Force Personnel with a Problem in the Past Year

	General Information (%)	Specific Information (%)	Advocate (%)	Advice, Coaching, Education (%)	Emotional or Social Support (%)	Professional Counseling (%)	Loans, Donations, or Help with Responsibilities (%)	Activities, Facilities (%)
1. Military practices and culture	18	14	12	16	5	6	1	3
2. Own well-being	6	5	5	14	17	15	3	14
3. Work-life balance	7	5	3	10	8	5	3	12

NOTE: N = 71,247 personnel.

42

As an example of how to read this table, focusing on the first cell, 18% of personnel who had problems in the military practices and culture problem type (the first row) expressed a need for general information (the first column). Specific examples of what issues are included in this type of problem are shown in Appendix D. Programs and resources that address the types of challenges associated with each problem type (i.e., each row) could use the information on the types of needs that Air Force personnel believed resulted from these types of problems to inform outreach efforts. For example, some experiencing problems with their own well-being perceived not just a need for emotional or social support (17%) or professional counseling (15%) but also advice, coaching or education (14%) and activities and facilities for activities (14%).

For each of the three problem types most common among spouses of airmen, Table 3.4 shows spouses' greatest self-reported needs. Among spouses facing past-year problems with their own well-being, 38% perceived no associated need for assistance; however, 25% felt they needed emotional or social support; 19% needed activities or facilities; and 17% felt they needed professional counseling. Among spouses dealing with military practices and culture problems, the most commonly selected needs were for specific information (27%) or general information (24%). This finding is not surprising, given that 46% of these spouses named "Getting accurate information about when your spouse will have to move, deploy, or travel for work" as one of the military practices and culture problems they experienced.[24]

_____

[24] For more information, see appendix Table D.6.

44

Table 3.4. Two Greatest Self-Reported Needs for the Top Three Types of Problems, Among Spouses with a Pro...

	General Information (%)	Specific Information (%)	Advocate (%)	Advice, Coaching, Education (%)	Emotional or Social Support (%)	Professional Counseling (%)	Loans, Donations, or Help with Responsibilities (%)	Activities, Facilities (%)
1. Own well-being	6	3	4	10	25	17	5	19
2. Work-life balance	6	3	2	8	13	6	6	18
3. Military practices and culture	24	27	12	10	8	3	2	7

NOTES: N = 6,708 spouses.

Exploring Variation in Responses: Sole or Most Significant Type of Problem

This section further explores the top problem type community members experienced in the past year, whether it was their sole problem type or the one among multiple problems they ranked as most significant. Knowledge of whether location or individual characteristics were associated with different types of top problems may help policymakers strategize how best to tailor outreach and programs to prevent or respond to problems.

Separate statistical models for airmen, employees, and spouses were used to examine location, military service and demographic characteristics associated with the selection and prioritization of different types of problems.[25] We thus explored whether individuals at certain types of locations, or with certain characteristics, showed different response patterns in terms of which problem type was their top type of problem.

As a reminder, the nine specified types of problems that community members could have selected as the top problem type they experienced in the past year were

- military practices and culture
- work-life balance
- household management
- financial or legal
- health care system
- romantic relationships
- child specific
- own well-being
- spouse or romantic partner's problems.

Also recall that Appendix B provides a complete list of the specific issues listed under each of these problem types. We did not explore characteristics associated with "other" as a top problem, given that this category includes a mixture of multiple problem types; it would thus be difficult to interpret the results. Note that child-specific questions and questions regarding spouse or romantic partner's problems were asked only of respondents who had indicated in the initial demographics questions that they had minor children or a spouse or partner.

As a threshold for the differences we report in this section, we first applied our stringent criteria for statistical significance of p <0.001. Next, for each characteristic in each model, we identified whether differences were found for at least three of the nine problem choices examined for each model (airman, spouse, or Air Force civilian employee) and, hence, bring to the foreground the characteristics that demonstrated a pattern of relevance.[26] We summarize these

---

[25] For technical readers, output with full model results is available from the authors.

[26] In other sections of the report, we were able to set further criteria for meaningfulness based on a magnitude of difference using translated odds ratios. However, for these analyses, the overall prevalence of individual problem

model results in greater detail here. As a reminder, *top problem* refers to the self-reported sole or most significant type of problem someone experienced in the past year. At the end of the summary for each model, we provide an overview table with a checkmark indicating each of the characteristics that met our criteria of statistically significant differences in responses for at least three of the nine problem types (shown in Table 3.5 for airmen, Table 3.6 for spouses of airmen, and Table 3.7 for civilian employees).

Airmen

Most military service and demographic characteristics considered were associated with top problem type using our criteria, but none of the location characteristics were (see Table 3.5). Controlling for other variables in the model, the following characteristics were associated with the top past year type of problem:

- **Marital status** was significantly related to several sole or prioritized problem types. By definition, only airmen with a spouse or partner reported that their own top problem related to their significant other's past-year problems. The models revealed additional differences. Compared with unmarried airmen who were not in committed romantic relationship,

    - Married airmen were *less* likely to report either their own well-being or financial or legal problems as their top problem.
    - Married airmen were *more* likely to have had health care system problems as a top problem.
    - Unmarried airmen in a committed relationship were *more* likely to report their own well-being as their top problem.

- **Having minor children** (under age 18) was associated with several top problem types. By definition, only airmen with minor children reported child-specific problems as their top problem. Compared with airmen without minor children, airmen with minor children were

    - *less* likely to choose spouse or partner's problems, military practices and culture, or their own well-being as their top problem
    - *more* likely to choose financial and legal problems.

- The **self-reported number of hours worked** by airmen was related to many top problem types. Compared with airmen who worked less than 40 hours a week,

---

choices in the models varied quite a bit (for example, among airmen with any problems, it ranged from 3% who selected household management to 24% who selected military practices and culture). The percentage-point differences that might be potentially meaningful differed as well. For example, a 3-percentage-point difference for a problem choice with a low overall prevalence, such as household management, might represent doubling the prevalence for the comparison group relative to the overall airman population. That same magnitude of difference would represent a much smaller change in prevalence for choice of military practices and culture as a top problem. Thus, we selected an alternative approach rather than setting a common threshold for percentage-point differences across problem types and models. For technical readers, output with full model results is available from the authors.

- Airmen working 40 to 49 hours a week and airmen working 50 or more hours a week were *more* likely to select military practice and culture problems.
- Airmen working 50 or more hours a week were *less* likely to report romantic relationship problems or their own well-being as their top problem.
- Airmen working 40 to 49 hours were *more* likely to have had health care system problems or their own well-being as their top problem.
- Work-life balance problems were *less* likely to be a top problem for airmen working 40–49 hours but *more* likely to be a top problem for airmen working 50 or more hours per week.

- **Component** was also significantly related top type of problem in the past year. Compared with active component airmen,

  - Guard members were *less* likely to report military practices and culture, health care system, or child-specific problems as their top problem.
  - Guard members were *more* likely to report household management as a top problem.
  - Both reserve and guard members were *more* likely than active component airmen to report financial and legal problems as a top problem.
  - Reserve airmen were *less* likely to highlight their own well-being as a top problem.

- **Rank group** was associated with many top problem types. Compared with junior enlisted,

  - Junior noncommissioned officers (NCOs) (E5–E6) were *more* likely to indicate that their top problem type was military practices and culture or financial and legal problems.
  - Senior NCOs were *more* likely to indicate that their top problem was their own well-being or health care system problems but *less* likely than junior enlisted to indicate that financial or legal problems were their top type of problem.
  - Both junior and senior officers were *more* likely than junior enlisted to indicate work-life balance was a top past-year type of problem and *less* likely to indicate that their own well-being or financial and legal problems were.

Table 3.5. Overview of Characteristics Associated with Notable Differences in Airmen's Top Type o

		Military Practices and Culture	Work-Life Balance	Own Well-Being	Household Management	Romantic Relationships	Health Care System	Financial or Legal
Location	U.S. or foreign							
	Remote and isolated							
	Non–Air Force–led installation							
	Somewhere other than an installation							
Military service	Component	✓		✓	✓		✓	✓
	Rank group	✓	✓	✓			✓	✓
	Military career group							
	Distance from base	✓	✓		✓			
	Personnel nights away from home							
	Personnel hours working Air Force duties	✓	✓	✓		✓	✓	
Demographic	Marital status			✓			✓	✓
	Minor child(ren)	✓		✓				✓

NOTES: *Top* refers to the sole type of problem experienced in the past year or to the type the respondent prioritized as most significant. These regre statistically significant differences (*p* <0.001) for characteristics with significant differences across at least three problem types, controlling for all othe individual demographic and military service characteristics.
[a] These spouse or partner and child-specific problem categories were asked only of airmen who had previously indicated in the demographics items partner or a minor child, respectively. Hence, only individuals who reported those demographic characteristics were included in analyses for these pr

Odds ratios were used to describe associations between individual characteristics and binary outcomes and were estimated using logistic regression models, weighted to account for survey nonresponse. Odds ratios can be difficult to interpret. To aid in interpretation, we translated odds ratios into minimum-percentage-point differences in the outcomes for the baseline and comparison group. As noted above, we looked for a pattern of findings to establish meaningfulness rather than setting a percentage difference cut point that might not be applicable to the full range of top problem types. This also helped resolve the issue of focusing on meaningfulness rather than simply statistical significance.[27] Here, we further highlight the largest differences to help provide greater insight into the magnitude of the associations. Rank was associated with reports of work-life balance as a top problem, such that both junior and senior officers had odds ratios of 1.6. Compared with junior enlisted airmen, officers were approximately 60% more likely to report this particular problem type as their sole or most significant.

Another example to illustrate the magnitude of differences is for financial and legal problems as the top problem type. Compared with active component airmen, being in the guard was associated with an increase of 3.4 times the odds of reporting financial and legal problems as their top problem type. Being in the reserve was also associated with an increase: Reserve airmen were approximately 110% more likely (odds ratio: 2.1). These findings suggest that, although the overall prevalence for selection of this type of top problem was low, an intervention aimed at the reserve component might be warranted.

Spouses of Airmen

Our sample of spouses was much smaller than our other samples, and the models for child well-being, spouse's own well-being, and household management had no characteristics that reached our stringent criteria for statistical significance of $p < 0.001$.[28] As a reminder, marital

---

[27] Sometimes, despite this precaution, differences that were statistically different were not necessarily meaningfully different, although they met our criteria for discussion. The smallest difference we found is an example. Working 40–49 hours a week, in contrast with working less than 40, was associated with a significant difference in reporting own well-being as a top problem type. The estimated odds ratio was 1.018. While the difference is statistically significant, it was associated with virtually no practical difference in the number of people working 40–49 hours a week who reported this as a top problem—approximately a 1% increase compared with those working less than 40 hours.

[28] We tested the potential implications of excluding the "airmen's rank group unknown" spouses from the models. Nearly all these spouses were also Air Force civilian employees; in total, they comprised about 11% of our spouse sample. For the most part, the results did not change substantively. However, removing rank group unknown spouses from the analysis changed two of our top problem selection models:

- The overall model for choice of spouse well-being became significant: Spouses of junior officers were less likely to select spouse well-being as a top problem than spouses of junior enlisted, and spouses whose airmen spent 30–179 nights away from home for military duties in the past year were less likely to select this top problem.

status was not included in the model for selection of spouse or partner's problems, and those without minor children were not included in the model for child-specific problems. Across the other problem types, two characteristics were noteworthy for reaching that level of statistical significance across at least three problem types. The characteristics were their airman's component, and the spouse's own employment status. An overview of our findings is also shown in Table 3.6, and we discuss these in more detail later.

Component accounted for several differences. Compared with spouses of active component airmen,

- Spouses of guard members were *more* likely to select work-life balance as a top problem.
- Spouses of guard members were *less* likely to select health care system problems as a top problem.
- Spouses of both guard and reserve airmen were *less* likely than spouses of active component airmen to choose military practices and culture as a top problem.

Spouse employment was also relevant. Compared with spouses who were not working full or part time (which includes self-employment),

- Employed spouses were *more* likely to select work-life balance or romantic relationships as a top problem and *less* likely to select their own well-being.

As with the airmen models, we discuss the range of what these effects might mean. The smallest effect discussed here was for the selection of romantic relationships (which for spouses refers to their marital relationship) as the top type of problem in the past year. Compared with spouses who were not employed, employed spouses were approximately 50% more likely to report this as a top problem (odds ratio 1.5).

The largest of the effects discussed above is the association between spouse's employment and selection of work-life balance as a top problem; being employed was associated with an approximate increase of 130% (odds ratio 2.3) in likelihood of selecting this problem over not being employed.

- For choice of military practices and culture, when unknown rank group was removed from the model, no rank group was significantly associated with choice of this top problem; moreover, in the revised model, spouses whose airmen spent 180 nights or more away from home for military duties were more likely to select this top problem.

Table 3.6. Overview of Characteristics Associated with Notable Differences in Spouses' Top Type c

		Military Practices and Culture	Work-Life Balance	Own Well-Being	Household Management	Romantic Relationships	Health Care System	Financial or Legal
Location	U.S. or foreign							
	Remote and isolated							
	Non–Air Force–led installation							
	Somewhere other than an installation							
Military service[a]	Component	✓	✓				✓	
	Rank group[b]							
	Distance from base							
	Personnel nights away from home							
	Personnel hours working Air Force duties							
Demographic	Spouse employment		✓	✓		✓		
	Minor child(ren)							

NOTES: *Top* refers to the sole type of problem experienced in the past year or to the type the respondent prioritized as most significant. These re statistically significant differences ($p < 0.001$) for characteristics with significant differences across at least three problem types, controlling for all o individuals' demographic and military service characteristics.

[a] In the spouse models, component, rank group, nights away from home, and hours working refer to their airmen's characteristics.

[b] Not asked of spouses who are also civilian employees.

[c] This child-specific problem category was asked only of spouses who had previously indicated in the demographics items that they had a minor c who reported that demographic characteristic were included in analysis for this problem type.

51

Civilian Employees

For Air Force civilian employees, three characteristics were relevant to the top problem type based on our criteria: their status as a veteran, their marital status, and the presence of minor children. An overview of these findings is shown in Table 3.7 and discussed in detail in the following discussion. Note that the model for predicting top spouse or partner problems only included married civilian employees as only they were asked about these problems; similarly, only employees who indicated they had minor children were asked about child-specific problems. Controlling for other factors included in the model, the following differences were observed:

- Veteran status was relevant. Compared with civilian employees who were not veterans, civilian employees who were military veterans were

  - *more* likely to select military practices and culture and health care system problems as a top problem
  - *less* likely to select work-life balance or financial or legal challenges as top problem types.

- Marital status was also important. By definition, only employees with a spouse or partner reported that their own top problem related to their significant other's past-year problems. Additionally, the models showed that, compared with civilian employees who were unmarried and not in a committed relationship,

  - Employees who were unmarried and in a committed relationship were *less* likely to report work-life balance as a top problem type but *more* likely to report their own well-being as a top problem.
  - Married employees were *less* likely to have had financial and legal challenges as a top problem.

- Compared with civilian employees without minor children, employees with minor children were

  - *more* likely to have had work-life balance or financial and legal challenges as their top problem type
  - *less* likely to select military practices and culture, health care system problems, their own well-being, and or their spouse's or partner's problems as the top type of problem they faced in the past year.

The smallest effect for the differences discussed above was for the selection of health care system problems as a top problem. Having minor children was associated with a decrease of approximately 30% (odds ratio of 0.7) in likelihood to select this as the top problem type.

Table 3.7. Overview of Characteristics Associated with Notable Differences in Civilian Employees' Top

		Military Practices and Culture	Work-Life Balance	Own Well-Being	Household Management	Romantic Relationships	Health Care System	Financial or Legal
Location	U.S. or foreign							
	Remote and isolated							
	Non–Air Force–led installation							
	Somewhere other than an installation							
Military service	Dual hat: both airman and employee							
	Veteran status	✓	✓					✓
	Employee type							
	Distance from base							
	Personnel hours working Air Force duties							
Demographic	Marital status	✓	✓	✓				✓
	Minor child(ren)		✓	✓				✓

NOTES: *Top* refers to the sole type of problem experienced in the past year or to the type the respondent prioritized as most significant. These re[g] statistically significant differences ($p < 0.001$) for characteristics with significant differences across at least three problem types, controlling for all o[f] individual demographic and military service characteristics.
[a] These spouse or partner and child-specific problem categories were asked only of civilian employees who had previously indicated in the demog[raphic] a spouse or partner or a minor child, respectively. Hence, only individuals who reported these demographic characteristics were included in analys[es].

53

The largest of the effects discussed above was the association of marital status with own well-being as a top problem. In comparison to unmarried employees not in a committed relationship, civilians who were similar but unmarried and in a committed relationship were approximately 40% more likely (odds ratio of 1.4) to report having a problem with their own well-being. This suggests that, in strategizing how best to support well-being among Air Force civilians, the Air Force must think not only in terms of married and unmarried employees but in terms of how having a nonmarital significant other may matter.

Findings and Conclusions

Although about 10% of Air Force personnel and 8% of spouses reported experiencing no problems in the past year, most community members did report facing challenges. When asked a broad question about the nature of these problems, the most frequently chosen categories across the community were problems of military practices and culture, work-life balance, and their own well-being. Respondents with issues in more than one of the problem categories were asked to indicate which single category of problem was the most significant. The categories most commonly chosen more generally were also those that remained after respondents with multiple problem types were asked to narrow theirs down to only the most significant. This was true for both personnel and spouses, although the distinction in frequencies between spouses' top three and the other types of problems was not as clear cut, and spouses also commonly noted health care system problems.

Within each of the three most commonly selected top problem types, we examined the specific issues commonly chosen by those for whom it was a top problem. For example, among personnel for whom work-life balance was their top type of problem, frequently reported issues were finding enough time for sleep, a healthy diet, or physical exercise (62%), as well as finding sufficient time for other self-care activities. As another example, 59% of Air Force personnel who selected military practices and culture as their top type of past-year problem indicated that one of the problems was poor leadership by the military chain of command. Among personnel who indicated that their top problem type was military practices and culture, more than 30% indicated that, at its worst, that type of problem was experienced as severe. On the lower end, only 19% of personnel whose top problems were financial or legal characterized them as severe at their worst.

Among community members who experienced problems in the past year, 40% of Air Force personnel and 33% of spouses reported not needing assistance for their top type of problem. Often, this was because they had already solved or were solving the problem themselves, but about 20% reported that it was because they believed there was nothing anyone could do to help.

Survey participants who experienced any problems in the past year were asked to indicate what *kinds* of help they or their families needed to deal with the type of problem they had prioritized as most significant or as their only type of problem. Frequently chosen categories of

54

needs included advice, coaching, or education and general information (among personnel) and general information and emotional or social support (among spouses).

We also looked at how these needs related to problem types, to further sharpen the focus. Among personnel, 18% who had problems of the military practices and culture problem type expressed a need for general information while 16% expressed a need for advice, coaching, or education. Among spouses, 25% of those who reported problems of their own well-being indicated a need for emotional and social support, while 19% reported a need for activities and facilities for activities. Relevant programs and resources could use the reported associations between top problems and the most pressing needs to focus on the most frequently paired needs in a constrained resource environment or to consider more broadly the array of needs that community members with a given problem type might be experiencing. This information could be used to inform program planning and outreach efforts.

We used statistical models to help Air Force leaders understand what location, demographic, and military service characteristics might be most closely associated with the type of problem community members found to be their most significant or only type of problem. Some characteristics were related to the same items in more than one of the three population groups (airmen, spouses of airmen who are not airmen themselves, and Air Force civilian employees). For example, for both airmen and civilian employees, having minor children was associated with multiple items, including being more likely to have had financial and legal challenges as a top problem and being less likely to report military practices and culture, their own well-being, or a spouse's or partner's problems as their own main challenge in the past year. This is understandable; having children can have wide-ranging effects on financial situations. The U.S. Department of Agriculture estimates that raising a child to adulthood of costs more than $200,000; for a middle-income family in 2015, the cost was more than $10,000 per child per year (Lino et al., 2017). Being married was associated with being less likely to choose financial and legal challenges for both employees and airmen; although we did not assess employment of airmen's spouses for personnel models, it seems possible this could be related to having another contributor to household income. Component was relevant for both airmen and their spouses. For example, compared with active component airmen and spouses, guard members and spouses were less likely to report top problems in the domains of military practices and culture or health care system.

Other associations were confined to a given subgroup. For example, the number of hours airmen worked influenced the likelihood of reporting military practices and culture problems; health care system problems; and, for those working 50 or more hours a week, work-life conflict. Given the military's role in managing workload and manpower and that perceptions of poor leadership were frequently reported issues among those whose top problem was military practices and culture, the association is not necessarily surprising. Similarly, a heavy workload may make it difficult to schedule and attend medical appointments, which can cause difficulty using the health care system. Officers were more likely than enlisted to choose work-life balance challenges as their top problems, indicating that this was a particular issue of concern for that subgroup. Junior enlisted and NCOs were more likely to choose financial and legal problems and military practices and culture problems than were other rank groups, potentially reflecting lower pay and/or lower positions within the organization.

In a finding that potentially parallels the association of higher workload and work-life balance problems among airmen, spouses who worked (whether full time or part time) were more likely to report work-life balance as their top problem; they were also less likely to select their own well-being as a top problem. This may be a reflection of the benefits associated with work or, conversely, that those who were not doing well were less likely to want or be able to work. Civilian employees who were military veterans were more likely to choose military practices and culture as a top problem. They were also more likely to select health care challenges as a top problem and less likely to select work-life balance or financial and legal challenges. Perhaps there was an adjustment factor at play, as former service members adapted to working as a civilian, not wearing rank, and having to navigate health care differently than before, but also gained relatively more control over their personal lives. Additionally, civilian employees who are military retirees may be in a particularly advantageous financial situation relative to their counterparts who are not.

Outreach to civilians, spouses, and airmen can both target the problem areas most likely to be selected as a top choice and focus in on particular demographic subgroups for intervention. For example, promotion of financial education and counseling services may target junior enlisted airmen, airmen in the reserve component, and unmarried airmen and civilian employees. Leadership initiatives to manage workload could focus on officers but also more locally on units in which working more than 40 hours a week is the norm.

4. Help-Seeking Behaviors Among Respondents with Needs

This chapter builds on the previous chapter by providing results on the follow-up questions asked of respondents who indicated that they had needed assistance related to their sole or most significant type of problem in the past year. For each of their greatest needs (one or two), the survey asked this subset of respondents to select from presented lists any of the types of resources they or their spouse or partner had contacted in the past year to try to meet this need.

Resources Contacted for Greatest Needs

For this subset of respondents, this section addresses what the population did about needs for assistance with that top type of problem:

- Who did nothing and why?
- What military resources did community members contact?
- What nonmilitary resources did community members contact?

Why Did Some Air Force Community Members Not Contact Anyone for Assistance with Their Needs?

Some personnel indicated that they did not contact anyone for help with their greatest needs. Overall, 13% of Air Force personnel and 13% of spouses with needs for their top type of problem did not contact any military or nonmilitary resources to help with one or both of their greatest needs.

Those who had needs for their top problem type but did not contact any resources were asked what the main reason was that they did not contact anyone for help with this need. The survey presented a list of possible reasons and permitted respondents to select one option for each need. Through this item, Air Force personnel reported the following reasons for not reaching out for one or both of their greatest needs:

- 19% said that they had already met the need themselves.
- 23% said that they were currently meeting the need themselves.
- 9% said the problem was fixed another way.
- 26% thought there was nothing anyone could do to help solve the problem.
- 21% did not want to ask for help.
- 18% did not know who to contact for help.

Among spouses who did not reach out for help, the results were similar, with the exception that a greater percentage of spouses (30%) did not know who to contact. Specifically,

- 17% said that they had already met the need themselves.
- 22% said that they were currently meeting the need themselves.

- 8% said the problem was fixed another way.
- 27% thought there was nothing anyone could do to help solve the problem.
- 19% did not want to ask for help.
- 30% did not know who to contact for help.

Which Military Resources Did Community Members Contact?

Although some community members did not contact anyone for help with their greatest needs for their top type of problem, some did. Table 4.1 shows the percentage of Air Force personnel and spouses with such needs who reached out to different types of *military* resources, in the order that the resources appeared on the survey. Note that not all military resources would apply or apply equally to all populations (e.g., some personnel live farther away from base than others; eligibility for some programs and services may vary). Across Air Force personnel and spouses, the chain of command, unit members or coworkers, military friends, and military spouses were among the military resources most commonly contacted for help. Among spouses, only 7% reached out the Air Force Key Spouse Program, which is a formal commander's unit readiness program whose mission is to provide information and resources to military spouses and thereby help support readiness and resilience (Air Force Personnel Center, 2018b). Notably, 33% of Air Force personnel and 39% of spouses did not contact any military individuals or resources for help with their needs.

Table 4.1. Military Resources Community Members Contacted for Self-Reported Greatest Needs for Their Top Type of Problem, Among Those with Such Needs

	Personnel Overall (%)	Spouses of Airmen (%)
Chain of command (CoC)	43	40
Unit members, coworkers, or military friends not in your CoC	42	34
Unit members/coworkers/military friends not in your spouse's CoC	27	27
Other military spouses who are civilians	30	28
Airman and Family Readiness Center or Military and Family Readiness Center	13	17
Family Assistance Center	4	3
Child and Youth Programs	7	10
Military hotline, or referral line	5	7
Military Internet resources or social media	11	17
Chaplain or other members of military religious or spiritual group	8	6
Mental health care provider	15	13
Medical or health care provider	18	20
Air Force Key Spouse Program	4	7
On-base Force Support Squadron resources	8	7
Resources for legal and policy violations	5	3
Other military contacts	9	11
Did not contact any military individuals or resources	33	39

NOTES: *N* = 41,812 personnel and 4,405 spouses who indicated their use of one or more resources. Only civilian employees who are also military spouses were asked about "other military spouses who are civilians." Only guard and guard spouses were asked about the Family Assistance Center. Only Air Force spouses and married airmen were asked about the Air Force Key Spouse Program. Only those with minor children were asked about Child and Youth Programs. Responses from civilian employees who are also spouses of airmen are included in both the personnel and spouse results. *Top* refers to the sole type of problem experienced in the past year or to the type the respondent prioritized as most significant.

Of the 15% of Air Force personnel and 13% of spouses who contacted one or more mental health care providers,

- 77% of the Air Force personnel and 59% of the spouses contacted a provider at an on-base mental health clinic, a military medical provider not in the mental health clinic (such as a primary care doctor or behavioral health provider), or a Director of Psychological Health.
- 30% of the personnel and 37% of the spouses contacted a Military and Family Life Counselor or a therapist referred by Military OneSource.
- 11% of the personnel and 20% of the spouses were not sure which type of mental health care provider they contacted.

The last finding is an important reminder that community members may not know local resources—even the ones they use—by the name of the program or office.

Which Nonmilitary Resources Did Community Members Contact?

Military resources are not the only sources of support for Air Force community members. The survey also showed respondents with needs a list of types of nonmilitary resources and asked them to indicate which they or their spouse or partner contacted to try to meet their needs. Table 4.2 shows the percentage of community members with needs for their top type of problem who reached out to different types of nonmilitary resources, also presented here in the order they appeared on the survey. The patterns were again somewhat similar across Air Force personnel and spouses, with both subgroups most commonly turning to personal networks outside the military and internet resources for help rather than professional service providers. Additionally, 52% of personnel and 44% of spouses did not contact any nonmilitary resources for assistance (compared with 33% of personnel and 39% of spouses who did not contact any *military* resources, as shown in Table 4.1).

Table 4.2. Nonmilitary Resources Community Members Contacted for Self-Reported Greatest Needs for Their Top Type of Problem, Among Those with Such Needs

	Personnel Overall (%)	Spouses of Airmen (%)
Resources for military or war veterans	6	5
Government or community resources for family services	4	6
Private clubs; organizations; or wellness, recreation, or fitness centers	9	13
Private off-base childcare	4	8
Civilian religious or spiritual group or leaders	11	13
Private mental health care provider	6	8
Private medical provider	10	12
Internet resources	24	33
Personal networks outside the military	32	40
Oversight authorities: governor, member of Congress, or other elected officials or their offices; resources for legal and policy violations[a]	5	4
Other nonmilitary contacts, including nonmilitary hotline, crisis line or referral line, civilian employer, labor union[a]	10	9
Did not contact any nonmilitary individuals or resources for help with this need	52	44

NOTES: *N* = 41,565 personnel and 4,391 spouses who indicated their use of one or more resources.
[a] Survey categories were combined to provide sufficient sample size to report these results more broadly across installations, and the same categories were retained here. Only guard and reserve were asked about civilian employers. Only employees were asked about labor unions. Responses from civilian employees who are also spouses of airmen are included in both the personnel and spouse results. *Top* refers to the sole type of problem experienced in the past year or to the type the respondent prioritized as most significant.

Perceived Effectiveness of Resources Used

From the perspective of community members who used resources, in this section, we examine how well resources were helping them with their greatest needs.

- How well did military resources help?
- How well did nonmilitary resources help?
- How many had unmet needs at the time of the survey?

How Well Did Military and Nonmilitary Resources Help?

Survey respondents who had reached out to any resources for help were asked to indicate how much each of these contacts helped meet whatever type of need the respondents had (e.g., for advice, coaching or education). Possible responses were that the contacts helped "a lot," "somewhat," "a little," or "not at all." Figure 4.1 displays Air Force personnel's ratings of how well military resources helped meet the needs for the respondents' top problem type. The figure shows all the types of military resources respondents could select, ordered by how the types were presented on the survey. The types and number of Air Force personnel rating each of these resources will vary because not all resources apply or apply equally to everyone. For example, Child and Youth Programs are relevant for only a specific subset of the population, but all airmen and employees have a chain of command they could have potentially contacted for assistance.

Mental health care providers and religious or spiritual resources were among those with the highest percentage of personnel feeling that these resources helped "a lot" with individual's greatest needs. On the other end of the spectrum, 36% of personnel who contacted Child and Youth Programs or resources for legal or policy violations felt these military resources did "not at all" help them meet their greatest need for their top past-year problem.

Figure 4.1. Air Force Personnel's Assessments of How Well Military Resources Contacted Were Able to Help with Greatest Needs for Their Top Type of Problem (%)

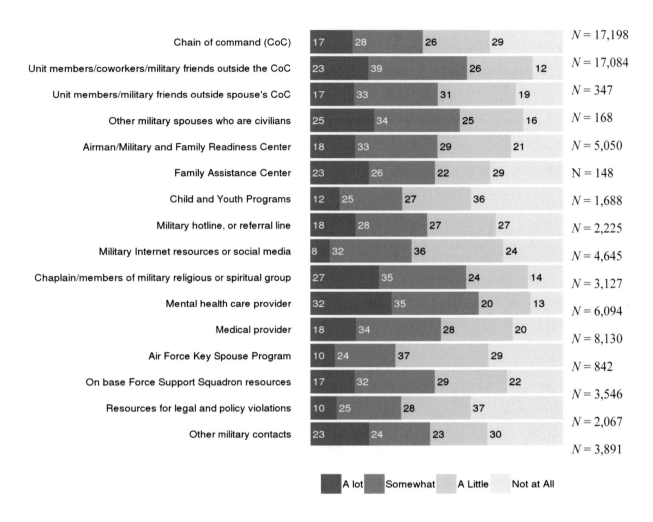

NOTES: *N* = 30,958 personnel who rated one or more resources. Figure includes only personnel who experienced problems in the past year, identified needs for their most significant type of problem, and reached out to at least one military resource for assistance. Only civilian employees who are also military spouses were asked about "other military spouses who are civilians." Only guard and guard spouses were asked about the Family Assistance Center. Only Air Force spouses and married airmen were asked about the Air Force Key Spouse Program. Only personnel with minor children were asked about Child and Youth Programs. *Top* refers to the sole type of problem experienced in the past year or to the type the respondent prioritized as most significant.

Figure 4.2 provides the same type of results for spouses of airmen who contacted military resources for assistance. As with Air Force personnel, mental health care providers and religious or spiritual resources were among those with the highest percentage of spouses feeling that these resources helped "a lot" with individuals' greatest needs (31% and 25%, respectively); here, other military spouses who are civilians were also at the top of this list (28%). On the negative side, 37% of spouses with minor children who contacted Child and Youth Programs and 34% of spouses who contacted the chain of command felt these military resources did "not at all" help them meet their greatest need for their top past-year problem. Although 37% of guard spouses who contacted the Family Assistance Center also felt not at all helped, we caution that that number is based on feedback from only 23 spouses.

Figure 4.2. Spouses' Assessments of How Well Military Resources Contacted Were Able to Help with Greatest Needs for Their Top Type of Problem (%)

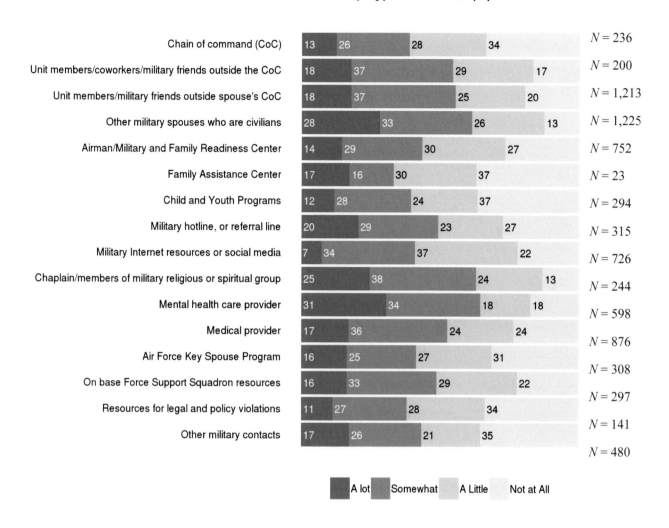

NOTE: *N* = 3,110 spouses who rated one or more resources. Figure includes only spouses who experienced problems in the past year, identified needs for their most significant type of problem, and reached out to at least one military resource for assistance. Only guard spouses were asked about the Family Assistance Center. Only spouses with minor children were asked about Child and Youth Programs. *Top* refers to the sole type of problem experienced in the past year or to the type the respondent prioritized as most significant.

Using the same question format, the survey also asked participants to tell us how much nonmilitary contacts help them meet their greatest needs. Figure 4.3 displays these results for Air Force personnel, also presented in the order they appeared on the survey. Personal networks were among those most commonly rated as helping "a lot" with Air Force personnel's needs for their top type of past-year problem, as were nonmilitary religious or spiritual resources and private mental health care and medical providers. Among the least helpful nonmilitary resources were government or political leaders (e.g., governor, member of Congress, elected officials): 47% of personnel who contacted them said they were "not at all" helpful.

Figure 4.3. Air Force Personnel's Assessments of How Well Nonmilitary Resources Contacted Were Able to Help with Greatest Needs for Their Top Type of Problem (%)

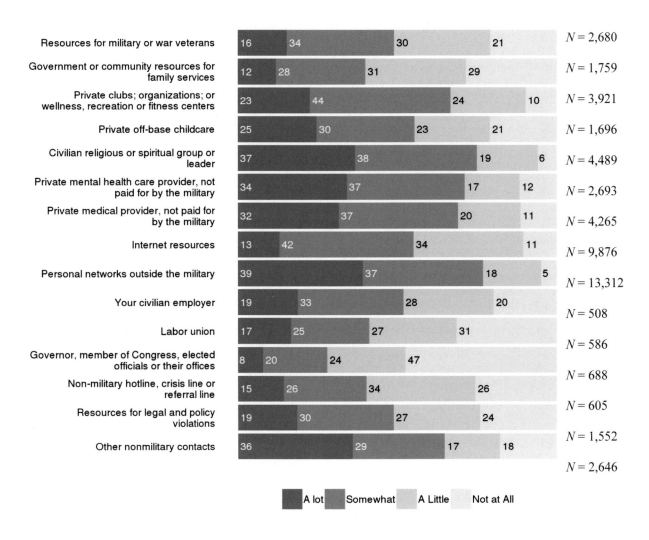

NOTE: *N* = 23,785 personnel who rated one or more resources. Figure includes only personnel in this community who experienced problems in the past year, identified needs for their most significant type of problem, and reached out to at least one nonmilitary resource for assistance. Only guard and reserve were asked about civilian employers. Only employees were asked about labor unions. *Top* refers to the sole type of problem experienced in the past year or to the type the respondent prioritized as most significant.

Figure 4.4 conveys the same type of information about nonmilitary resources contacted as provided by spouses. As with Air Force personnel, spouses' personal networks were among those most commonly rated as helping "a lot" with their top type of problem, as were nonmilitary religious or spiritual resources and private mental health care and medical providers. Also, similar to Air Force personnel, 50% of spouses of airmen who contacted government or political leaders found them to be "not at all" helpful.

Figure 4.4. Spouses' Assessments of How Well Nonmilitary Resources Contacted Were Able to Help with Greatest Needs for Their Top Type of Problem (%)

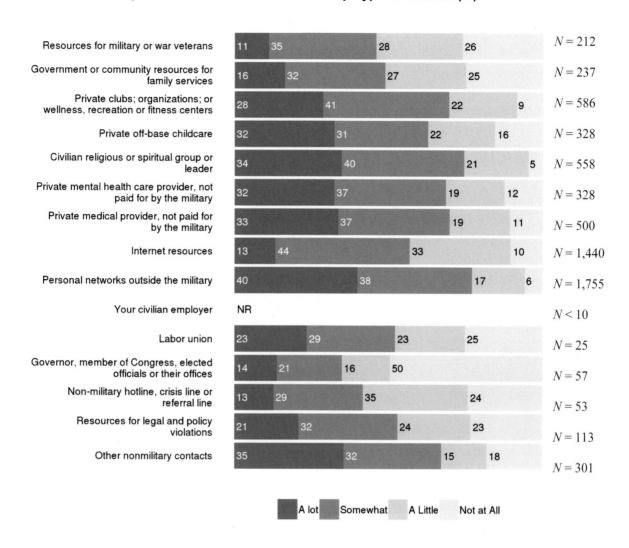

NOTE: *N* = 2,927 spouses who rated one or more resources. "NR" means "not reportable" because fewer than 10 spouses answered the question. Only spouses who were also guard or reserve were asked about civilian employers. Only spouses who were also Air Force employees were asked about labor unions. *Top* refers to the sole type of problem experienced in the past year or to the type the respondent prioritized as most significant.

Did Community Members Believe Their Greatest Needs Were Met?

Respondents who contacted anyone (military or nonmilitary) for help with their needs were asked this question: "In general, were you able to get the help you needed for these problems?" Response options were "yes," "no," or "not sure." We refer to those who said that they were able to get the help they needed as having had their *needs met*. We refer to those who said that they

65

were unsure or that they were not able to get the help they needed as having *unmet needs*. [29] Figure 4.5 indicates Air Force personnel's perceptions of whether, at the time of the survey, they had been able to get the help they needed for their top type of problem in the past year. Note that this presents Air Force personnel's perceptions of their ability to get help, which may not necessarily align with professional assessments. Still, members' own assessments shape their actions and attitudes.

Figure 4.5 shows that only 24% of personnel whose primary type of problem related to military practices and culture and who reached out for assistance felt their needs had been met. This contrasts sharply with the more than 50% of personnel who experienced several other types of problems (household management, romantic relationship, child-specific, own well-being, spouse or romantic partner's problems) who felt their needs were met.

Overall, 58% of Air Force personnel with at least one problem in the past year who contacted someone for assistance reported that they had unmet needs, despite reaching out.

Figure 4.6 shows the percentage of Air Force personnel with at least one unmet need by subgroup.

---

[29] It is possible that, at the time of the survey, some respondents were still in the process of solving a problem and that it was too soon for them to tell whether the assistance they were receiving would ultimately help them resolve their problem. For example, they may have just reported a problem to an authority figure or have just begun counseling or a medical treatment. Thus, "unmet needs" does not equal "never met needs."

Figure 4.5. Among Air Force Personnel Who Contacted a Resource for Help, Were Needs for Their Top Type of Problem Met? (%)

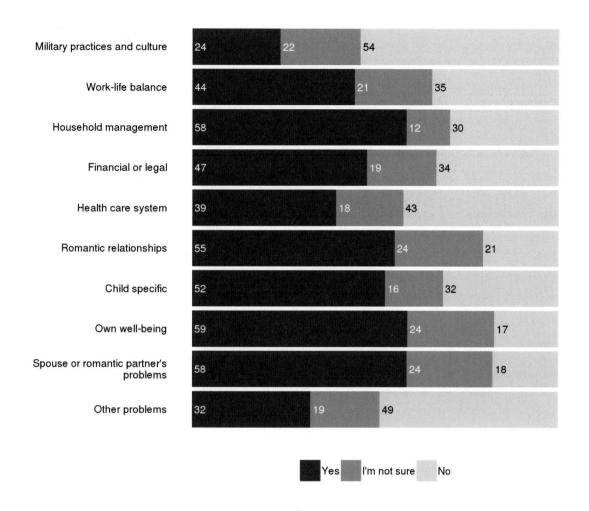

NOTE: *N* = 35,897 personnel (across all rows in the figure). *Top* refers to the sole type of problem experienced in the past year or to the type the respondent prioritized as most significant. This figure includes only personnel who experienced problems in the past year, identified needs for their top type of problem, and reached out to at least one military or nonmilitary resource for assistance. We refer to personnel who selected "I'm not sure" or "no" as having *unmet needs*.

Figure 4.6. Unmet Needs Among Air Force Personnel Who Contacted a Resource for Help with Their Top Problem, by Subgroup

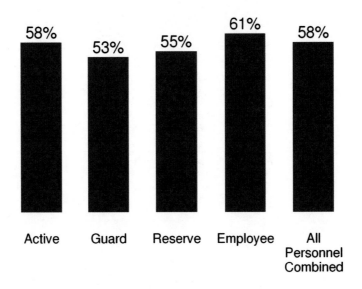

NOTE: Responses from individuals who are both airmen and employees are included in both subgroups' results. *Top* refers to the sole type of problem experienced in the past year or to the type the respondent prioritized as most significant. This figure includes only personnel who experienced problems in the past year, identified needs for their top type of problem, and reached out to at least one military or nonmilitary resource for assistance. Percentages reflect those who said that they were not able to get the help they needed or were unsure whether they had.

Figure 4.7 shows spouses' perceptions of whether or not they were able to get the help they needed for their top type of problem. As with Air Force personnel, 50% or more of spouses who reached out for assistance for several types of problems felt their greatest needs had been met. Specifically, this was true for problems regarding work-life balance, household management, and their own well-being and child-specific problems. This leaves substantial and noteworthy minorities of the spouses who did reach out who did not feel their needs had been met.

These figures present unmet needs for at least one of the needs community members indicated for their top type of problem, regardless of the problem type and help desired. This measure of unmet need shown in Figures 4.5 through 4.7 counts only those in the community who indicated they had needs for their top type of problem and that they reached out to obtain help solving their problems. This measure highlights vulnerable populations—those who have sought help but did not believe they received the help they needed. These figures are not representations of everyone with unmet needs. As reported earlier, some in the community did not reach out to resources, despite having needs for their top problem type, and the survey asked them why. Some of the answers suggested that they did not perceive an unmet need—for example, the problem went away on its own or was being solved. However, those who did not reach out for assistance with their needs because they felt there was nothing anyone could do, did not know who to contact for help, or did not want to ask for help may also have had an unmet need. Finally, personnel with more than one type of problem may have had unmet needs for other types of problems beyond the type they indicated was most significant. Thus, it is important to recognize that the portrayal of unmet needs here is very conservative and likely underestimates the amount of unmet need in the community.

Figure 4.7. Among Spouses Who Contacted a Resource for Help, Were Needs for Their Top Type of Problem Met? (%)

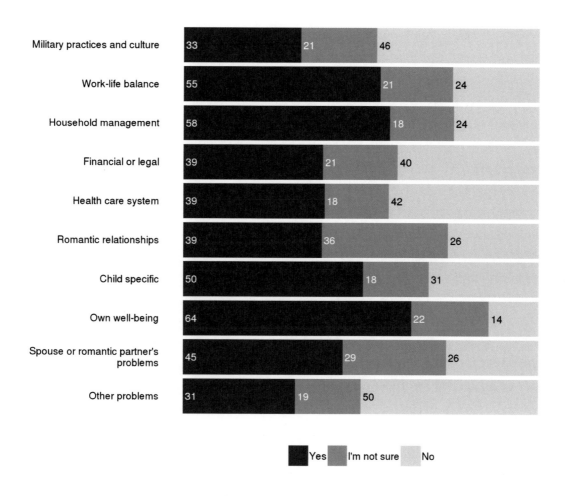

NOTE: *N* = 3,808 spouses. *Top* refers to the sole type of problem experienced in the past year or to the type the respondent prioritized as most significant. We refer to spouses who selected "I'm not sure" or "no" as having *unmet needs*.

Exploring Variation in Responses: Unmet Needs Among Those Who Reached Out for Assistance

As in our other statistical models, we used similar sets of relevant characteristics for each subgroup, with some modifications pertinent to each population, as described in Table 1.3. However, the models examined here address one of the components of the problem-solving status variable, so we did not include problem-solving status in our model because of its inherent redundancy.

The item selected in this chapter for further exploration is whether the respondent had **unmet needs**, which, again, was those someone who had reached out for help but felt unable to get the help they needed or were unsure whether they had. Those who did not reach out for help are not included in these models.

Previous research has demonstrated that unmet needs can have a meaningful effect on attitudes (Sims et al., 2017). More generally, this item was considered key for the simple fact that it highlights potentially vulnerable populations—those with unresolved problems. These are the community members Air Force providers and community planners have not (as yet) been able to help, and awareness of what factors influenced this status is relevant to addressing the needs of these types of individuals in the future.

The overall prevalence of unmet needs among those who had reached out to resources for help was similar across demographic subgroups and varied from 54% (for spouses) to 59% (for civilian employees). Given this similarity, we used a common cut point to highlight potentially meaningful differences in the odds ratios (in addition to the application of our criteria for statistical significance of p <0.001). Because this prevalence was relatively high, we set a minimum odds ratio corresponding to a minimum-percentage-point difference of 5% as a threshold for highlighting characteristics significantly associated with higher or lower likelihood of self-reporting unmet needs. By this, we mean we do not call attention to differences between two groups that are statistically significant but differ by only a few percentage points.[30]

Airmen

Table 4.3 presents the characteristics that met both criteria for statistical significance and magnitude of difference for the airmen model. Controlling for all other characteristics in the model, these factors were related to an increase in reports of unmet needs:

- Airmen living more than 30 minutes away from base were approximately 30% more likely to have had unmet needs than airmen living on base (odds ratio equal to 1.3).
- Airmen working 50 or more hours a week (compared with working less than 40 hours) were approximately 90% more likely to have had unmet needs (odds ratio equal to 1.9).
- Airmen spending 180 nights or more away from home in the past year because of military duties (in contrast to 0–30 nights) were approximately 30% more likely to have had unmet needs (odds ratio equal to 1.3).

We noted career group differences as well. Compared with airmen in the operations career group, there was one category of airmen who were approximately 20% less likely to report their needs unmet. This category combined airmen from across the smaller professional career group (legal and chaplain), special investigations career group, and airmen holding special duty

---

[30] For technical readers, output with full model results is available from the authors.

identifiers (e.g., recruiters, first sergeants, instructors, honor guard). These encompass many of the occupations or positions not open to new enlistees (including chaplain assistant, special investigations, recruiters, first sergeants) (U.S. Air Force, 2015), so this result may be picking up on an issue of organizational tenure and expertise or authority not otherwise captured in our model through the rank group variable.

Table 4.3. Overview of Characteristics Associated with Notable Differences in Unmet Needs for Top Past-Year Problem, Among Airmen Who Reached Out for Assistance

		Unmet Needs
Location	U.S. or foreign	
	Remote and isolated	
	Non–Air Force–led installation	
	Somewhere other than an installation	
Military service	Component	
	Rank group	
	Military career group	✓
	Distance from base	✓
	Personnel nights away from home	✓
	Personnel hours working Air Force duties	✓
Demographic	Marital status	
	Minor child(ren)	

NOTE: *Top* refers to the sole type of problem experienced in the past year or to the type the respondent prioritized as most significant.

Spouses of Airmen

Only one characteristic examined in the model for spouses that was statistically significantly associated with unmet needs and met our magnitude of difference criteria as well. Controlling for all other characteristics in the model,

- Being married to an airman who typically worked 50 or more hours a week for their Air Force duties (compared with married to an airman who typically works less than 40 hours per week) was associated with an *increase* in unmet needs: The odds ratio of 1.7 means that spouses who reported their airmen working these hours were approximately 70% more likely to have had unmet needs.

Civilian Employees

Only one characteristic we examined in the Air Force civilian employee model met our criteria for being associated with both statistically and substantially differences in reporting unmet needs. Compared with civilian employees who worked less than 40 hours a week,

- Working 50 or more hours a week was associated with an increase in unmet needs: The odds ratio of 2.1 means that civilians who reported they typically work 50 or more hours a week were approximately 110% more likely to report that they had not received the help they needed.

Findings and Conclusions

Not all community members who believed they needed help with their top type of problem reached out to military or nonmilitary resources for assistance. Indeed, about 10% did not reach out to any resources. Community members that did reach out to military resources most often reported contacting the chain of command or other military coworkers or friends. Of institutional sources of help outside the chain of command, mental and medical health care providers were sought by many. Some community members also reached out to nonmilitary resources for assistance, although reaching out to military resources was more prevalent. The most frequent nonmilitary resources contacted were personal networks and internet resources.

Those who contacted any resources were also asked how well those resources were able to help. Military mental health care providers and chaplains or other members of military religious or spiritual groups were most likely to be rated by community members as helping "a lot," and spouses were also most likely to rate other spouses as helping "a lot." Still, even for these most helpful resources, only 25–32% of personnel or spouses who contacted them rated the resources as helping "a lot." Air Force personnel tended to be less likely to say that military internet resources or social media, the Air Force Key Spouse Program, or military resources for legal and policy violations helped "a lot." Child and Youth Programs not only had relatively few who contacted them saying they helped "a lot" but a relatively high proportion saying they helped "not at all." Unfortunately, spouses of airmen reported a similarly low success rate with Child and Youth Programs, military internet or social media, and resources for legal and policy violations—with relatively few reporting that these resources helped "a lot" and relatively many reporting they helped "not at all." Moreover, a large proportion of spouses (31%) also reported the Air Force Key Spouse Program as helping "not at all."

Compared with the results for military resources in general, more Air Force personnel reported favorable results with nonmilitary resources. The nonmilitary resources with the greatest percentage reporting that they helped "a lot" were personal networks with people outside the military (39%), civilian religious contacts (37%), and private medical providers (32%). Conversely, however, 47% of those who reached out to government officials, such as their governor or congressional representative, found that they helped "not at all."

We asked community members who reached out for help whether their needs had been met for the type of problem they indicated was their sole or most significant in the past year. Overall, 57% of Air Force personnel with at least one problem in the past year who contacted someone for assistance reported that they had unmet needs, despite reaching out. We examined how this related to the different problem types reported as community members' top problem. Among personnel with military practices and culture problems, 54% indicated their corresponding needs were not met. In contrast, the majority of personnel whose top problem types were their own well-being, household management, or their spouses' or partners' problems indicated that their needs *were* met (59%, 58%, and 58%, respectively). The most frequent problem type for which spouses reported not having their needs met after reaching out was military practices and culture. However, majorities indicated that their needs were met when their top problem type was their own well-being, household management, or work-life balance (64%, 58%, and 55% respectively).

We also asked those who did not reach out for assistance with their needs why they did not. Although varying reasons for this were reported, 26% of personnel in this group said one reason was because there was nothing anyone could do. Moreover, 18% of personnel and 30% of spouses said they were not sure who to contact, which suggests that ongoing outreach and information campaigns might be helpful to inform community members of their options.

The findings suggest some key characteristics that can be used to help identify airmen, spouses, and Air Force civilians who sought help but were unable to meet their needs through available resources. The results provide the opportunity to use this information to focus in on community members more likely to have unmet needs. For airmen, these characteristics include living 30 or more minutes away from base and spending 180 nights or more in a given year away from home due to Air Force duties, such as deployments, temporary duties, training, and field exercises. As with findings regarding choice of top problems, a high workload can be influential in whether or not personnel get their needs met when they do reach out. Airmen and Air Force civilian employees who work 50 or more hours per week and the spouses whose airmen who bear a similar workload appear also to be particularly vulnerable.

This suggests that interventions that alleviate heavy workloads that necessitate working 50 or more hours a week could have an effect across the Air Force community and could facilitate meaningful differences in the numbers of community members who are able to resolve their problems, whether by alleviating the consequences of such a workload or allowing personnel the time to fully leverage the resources provided. It is not enough to raise awareness of programs and services: Community members must be able to access them, including having time in the day to do so.

5. Community Feedback on Military Resources

Chapter 4 reported responses regarding military and nonmilitary resources, but the findings came solely from those who reached out for help with their greatest needs for their top problem in the past year. It is also helpful to know the perceptions of military resources among all airmen, civilian employees and spouses, not just a particular subset of resource seekers. This chapter addresses the following questions:

- What were community members' perceived attributes of military resources?
- What was the members' level of ease or comfort with using military resources?
- What did the members anticipate would be the effects of not having the military resources available to help?
- How would Air Force personnel and spouses like to receive information about military resources?

It is important to keep in mind that respondent's ratings may have been influenced by word of mouth or experiences at locations other than their assignment at the time of the survey. But regardless of the reasons for them, these perceptions matter because perceptions can shape willingness to contact such resources in the future.

Perceived Attributes of Military Resources

All survey respondents were asked to review a list of military resources they may or may not have ever contacted for help with problems or life challenges and to "please select all statements that describe how you feel today about current resources." Table 5.1 displays the percentage of Air Force personnel who affirmed through the survey that various statements apply to different military resources, and Table 5.2 is the equivalent for spouses. Note that we cannot infer the opinions of those who did not affirm an item because they would include respondents who skipped the item, those who would not agree with the item, and those who had no opinion or mixed opinions.[31]

---

[31] Rather than presenting items in yes-or-no format, which would either clutter the survey screens or significantly add to the number of screens required for completion, these items were checkboxes. Thus, while checking an item meant a clear affirmative response to the sentiment that a resource has a "good reputation" (for example), the absence of marking this option does not mean that they actively disagreed.

Table 5.1. Percentage of Air Force Personnel Who Agreed with Descriptions of Various Resources

	Resource has a good reputation (%)	I know little to nothing about them (%)	Close or easy to access (%)	Might hurt my (or my spouse or partner's) reputation to use them for help (%)	Wait list or response time too long (%)
CoC	48	11	31	13	4
Airman (or Military) and Family Readiness Center	50	22	27	2	2
Family Assistance Center	41	36	20	2	2
Child and Youth Programs	29	45	17	1	5
Military hotline or referral line	31	42	21	2	2
Military Internet resources or social media	30	36	28	2	2
Chaplain or other members of military religious or spiritual group	52	20	28	2	1
Mental health care provider	39	25	24	11	4
Medical or health care provider	41	14	27	3	18
Air Force Key Spouse Program	29	46	19	4	2
On-base Force Support Squadron resources	42	19	36	1	4
Resources for legal and policy violations	36	33	25	3	3
Support services for victims of violence	50	20	30	2	1

NOTES: N = 76,916 personnel. Only guard and guard spouses were asked about the Family Assistance Center. Only Air Force spouses and married airmen were asked about the Air Force Key Spouse Program. The reputation item was worded, "Might hurt my reputation to contact them for help" for respondents without spouses or romantic partners and "Might hurt my or my spouse's/partner's reputation to contact them for help" for those who were married or in a committed relationship.

The list of resources matches the previous lists of military resources, with the exception of the addition of support services for victims of violence. Note that not all resources would apply or apply equally to all populations. As noted earlier, unmarried airmen would be unlikely to rely on the Key Spouse Program for assistance with their own personal needs. However, they may be aware of it and consider it as a resource for other reasons. These airmen may have been married in the past, may have heard about the program indirectly, or may interact with it as a part of their duties (e.g., in helping to integrate new arrivals on base, disseminate information about deployments to family members, or advertise activities or programs open to family members).

Table 5.1 shows that roughly 50% of surveyed personnel believed each of the following resources has a good reputation:

- the chain of command
- Airman (or Military) and Family Readiness Centers

- chaplains or other members of military religious or spiritual groups
- support services for victims of violence.

These were the military resources that the highest percentage of personnel agreed have a good reputation.

The military resources least likely to gain this good reputation endorsement were

- Child and Youth Programs
- military hotlines or referral lines (such as Military OneSource or Military Crisis Line)
- military internet resources or social media
- among married airmen, the Air Force Key Spouse Program.

About 30% of the respondents reported that these have a good reputation. However, it is important to note that more than 40% of personnel knew little to nothing about Child and Youth Programs or about military hotlines and referral lines, and more than 40% of married airmen knew little to nothing about the Air Force Key Spouse Program. Thus, in these cases, the low level of endorsement may be more of a lack of awareness of the resource than particularly poor reputations. Additionally, personnel without children or whose children are ineligible for Child and Youth Programs, such as on-base childcare or youth sports activities, may know little to nothing about them because they have not needed to inquire.

Other, more commonly applicable resources for a broader population or broader range of issues show a different awareness pattern: Relatively few personnel reported that they knew little to nothing about their chain of command (11%); medical or health care provider (14%); or on-base Force Support Squadron resources, such as those for food and dining, fitness, lodging, and entertainment (19%).

For all but one military resource, less than 32% of Air Force personnel would describe them as close or easy to access. The exception was on-base Force Support Squadron resources; 36% agreed these were close or easy to access. Perhaps especially notable is low endorsement of the military hotline or referral line (21%) and military internet resources or social media (28%), given the ubiquity of smartphones and that such resources can be accessed privately and outside of working hours.[32]

Asked to rate whether using any of these resources might hurt their (or their spouse or partner's) reputation, fewer than 5% felt that way for all resources but two: 11% thought there might be reputational consequences for seeing a mental health care provider, and 13% thought it might be harmful to contact the chain of command for help with problems or life challenges. Regarding another potential barrier to access, 5% or fewer personnel rated any of the military resources as having a wait list or response time that is too long, with the exception being that 18% indicated that this description fit medical or health care providers.

---

[32] Military OneSource, Safe Helpline, and the Military Crisis Line all offer 24/7 access to support via phone call or online chat.

Spouses' feedback (Table 5.2) shows an overall pattern of fewer agreeing that military resources have a good reputation and more expressing unfamiliarity with resources. This is not surprising, given that, for nearly 90%, the Air Force is not their direct employer.[33] The table shows that 40% of spouses believed the Airman (or Military) and Family Readiness Center has a good reputation; followed by 33% who said the same for the chain of command; and 33% who agreed that this also describes medical or health care providers, such as primary care doctors, nurses, nutritionists, and dentists. For all other military resources, 25% or fewer spouses rated the resources as having a good reputation.

Table 5.2. Percentage of Spouses Who Agreed with Descriptions of Various Resources

	Resource has a good reputation (%)	I know little to nothing about them (%)	Close or easy to access (%)	Might hurt my (or my spouse or partner's) reputation to use them for help (%)	Wait list or response time too long (%)
CoC	33	41	14	17	2
Airman (or Military) and Family Readiness Center	40	38	20	2	3
Family Assistance Center	21	67	7	2	1
Child and Youth Programs	24	55	12	1	8
Military hotline or referral line	20	62	12	2	2
Military Internet resources or social media	25	47	25	2	1
Chaplain or other members of military religious or spiritual group	31	50	15	3	1
Mental health care provider	21	52	13	11	4
Medical or health care provider	33	27	22	3	19
Air Force Key Spouse Program	24	59	12	4	3
On-base Force Support Squadron resources	31	44	24	0	3
Resources for legal and policy violations	21	62	13	2	3
Support services for victims of violence	24	61	13	2	1

NOTES: *N* = 7,103 spouses. Only guard spouses were asked about the Family Assistance Center. The reputation item was worded, "Might hurt my or my spouse's/partner's reputation to contact them for help."

Among guard spouses, 67% knew little to nothing about the guard's Family Assistance Center, and among all spouses, more than 60% said they knew little to nothing about military hotlines or referral lines; resources for legal and policy violations; and support services for

---

[33] For more information, see appendix Table B.7.

victims of violence, such as sexual assault or domestic violence. Moreover, 59% of spouses were unfamiliar with the Air Force Key Spouse Program; 54% were unfamiliar with Child and Youth Programs; 50% were unfamiliar with military chaplains or other members of military religious or spiritual groups and 51% were unfamiliar with military mental health care providers. Although there is a continuous stream of new spouses to orient to Air Force and other military resources, these results suggest there still may be room to make more spouses aware of the resources available to support them and their families. In terms of access, the resources that had the highest percentage of spouses rating them as close or easy to access were on-base Force Support Squadron resources (24%) and military internet resources or social media, such as Air Force or DoD web pages, base Twitter accounts, and official Facebook groups (25%). As with Air Force personnel, spouses' concerns about the potential harm to their or their airmen's reputation that might arise from using a resource was greatest for the chain of command (17%) and a mental health care provider (11%). For all other resources, 4% or fewer had that concern. Finally, as with Air Force personnel, the one type of military resource that stood out as having a wait list or long response time was the category of medical and health care providers.

Ease or Comfort with Using Military Resources

In the previous section, we described the items that asked community members to indicate whether certain attributes described specific types of military resources. But a wide range of local, Air Force, and DoD programs and services provides support to airmen, civilian employees, and spouses of airmen. Moreover, these resources can change names, locations, services, policies, eligibility, staff, and other particulars. Additionally, individuals may not seek out or retain information about resources that can help them until a particular need arises. Thus, it may be particularly valuable for members to possess a general level of comfort using military resources coupled with the knowledge of where to go if they find themselves needing assistance.

The survey asked all respondents to indicate the extent they agree with a set of statements about military resources for Air Force personnel and their families in general. Figures 5.1 and 5.2 show the exact wording of each of these statements as they appeared in the survey. Figure 5.1 displays the percentage of Air Force personnel who agreed or disagreed with these statements about their ease in finding out about or comfort with using military resources. Among airmen (and any civilian employees who are also spouses of airmen), 75% believed that it is easy to find out about military resources for airmen and their families. For the three other items, the majority of all personnel (airmen and civilian employees combined) agreed or strongly agreed that they know who to contact to find the right military resources when they have a problem (68%) or if military resources are not meeting their needs (58%) and that they are comfortable using military resources available to them (64%). However, a sizable minority of personnel (23–37%) either were neutral or did not agree with such statements.

78

Figure 5.1. Agreement with Ease or Comfort Using Military Resources, Among Air Force Personnel (%)

It is easy to find out about military resources for Airmen and their families.

When I have a problem finding the right military resource for my needs, I know who contact to find help.

If military resources are not meeting my needs, I know who to contact.

I am comfortable using military resources available to me.

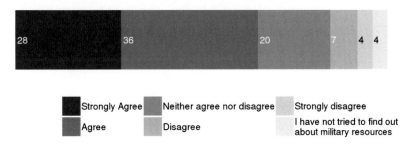

NOTE: *N* = 74,466 personnel. Only airmen and spouses of airmen were asked about the ease of finding out about military resources for airmen and their families.

Among spouses of airmen, a smaller percentage reported ease in finding out about or comfort using military resources (see Figure 5.2). Additionally, 48% felt it was easy to find out about military resources for them and their families; 41% said they knew who to contact if they had a problem finding the right military resource for their needs; and 34% reported knowing who to contact if military resources were not meeting their needs. Additionally, 50% were comfortable using military resources available to them. Note that about 9% of the spouses did not provide feedback on the ease or comfort of using military resources because they had not tried to find out about them.

Figure 5.2. Agreement with Ease or Comfort Using Military Resources, Among Spouses of Airmen (%)

It is easy to find out about military resources for Airmen and their families.

When I have a problem finding the right military resource for my needs, I know who contact to find help.

If military resources are not meeting my needs, I know who to contact.

I am comfortable using military resources available to me.

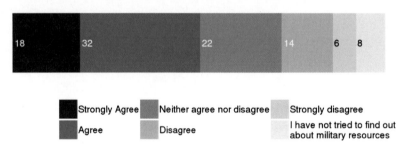

NOTE: N = 6,982 spouses.

Perceived Impact of a Resource No Longer Being Available

The survey asked community members, "What impact, if any, might there be if the following military resources were not available to help you address any problems you or your family might face?" followed by a list of types of military resources. Respondents also had the option of indicating that they did not believe the resource was currently available to them. Community members may or may not be able to accurately predict the actual impact; however, this approach helps convey the perceived value of these resources. Figure 5.3 displays the percentage of Air Force personnel who perceived a serious impact, some impact, or little to no impact if each resource was no longer available to them or their families. Figure 5.4 displays the same type of information from spouses of airmen. Among both personnel and spouses, the greatest anticipated impact would be if health care were no longer available or if their chain of command were no longer available to help them or their families address their problems.

Figure 5.3. Perceived Impact If Military Resources Were No Longer Available to Help Them or Their Families Address Problems, Among Air Force Personnel (%)

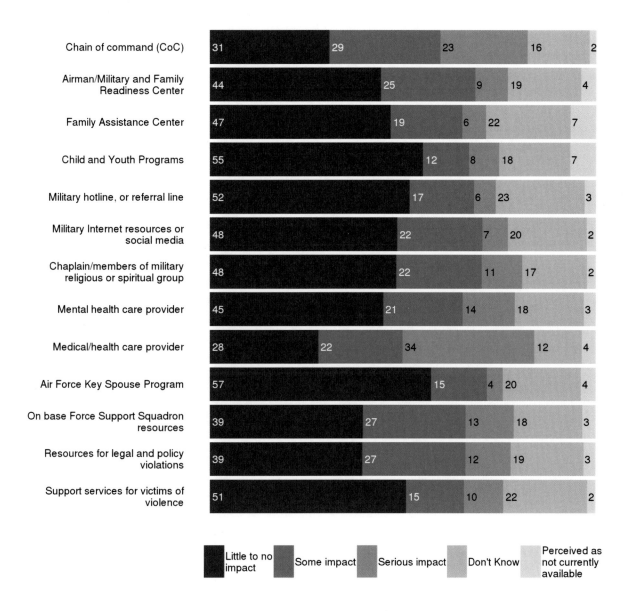

NOTE: *N* = 71,872 personnel rated one or more resources. Only guard and guard spouses were asked about the Family Assistance Center. Only Air Force spouses and married airmen were asked about the Air Force Key Spouse Program.

81

Figure 5.4. Perceived Impact If Military Resources Were No Longer Available to Help Them or Their Families Address Their Problems, Among Spouses (%)

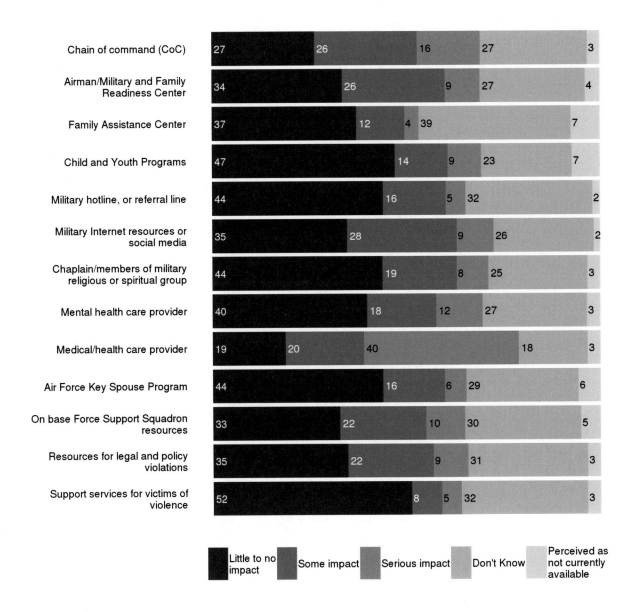

NOTES: *N* = 6,804 spouses rated one or more resources. The spouse version of the chain-of-command items referred specifically to the airman's chain of command. Only guard and guard spouses were asked about the Family Assistance Center. Only Air Force spouses and married airmen were asked about the Air Force Key Spouse Program.

Preferred Means of Receiving Information About Services

Thus far, this chapter has described community members' perceptions of military services, including which ones individuals know little to nothing about (Tables 5.1 and 5.2) and their ease or comfort in finding out about such services (Figures 5.1 and 5.2). There were also small minorities who believed that certain resources were not currently available to them (Figures 5.3 and 5.4), which, in some cases, could signal lack of awareness rather than lack of access.

Air Force leaders strategizing about ways to raise awareness of existing resources, remove barriers to access, and implement new initiatives will likely wish to consider which means of communication community members might prefer the Air Force use for news and outreach.

The survey asked respondents the following: "What is the best way for the Air Force to get information to you about services available to help meet your needs?" It allowed respondents to select all the means that applied. Preferences for unit leader emails to Air Force email addresses (54%) and to personal email addresses (32%) top the list. Figure 5.5 shows the most and least common ways that Air Force personnel want to receive information about services available to them, by subgroup. The preference for sending information to a personal email account makes particular sense for guard and reserve members, who infrequently have access to their official Air Force email account (e.g., drill weekends). Not everyone may be comfortable providing their personal email address to their chain of command or wish to receive official Air Force communication through both their personal and official email address, but clearly, some actually prefer it over other forms of communication. Among airmen, about 25% prefer learning about available resources through face-to-face communication, suggesting this form of communication should not be dropped in favor of solely electronic or other forms of mass communication. Installation newspapers and television announcements were among airmen's least commonly favored forms of communication. Although we did not test for statistically significant differences across demographic subgroups, Figure 5.5 suggests that preferences may vary by subgroup. There may be local preferences as well. For example, we observed that "TV" (television) appears higher on the list (in the 18–20% range) at some of the overseas locations, where some personnel and their families watch the Armed Forces Network for access to U.S. television programming. In place of commercials, the Armed Forces Network airs messaging from the military (e.g., events, tips, announcements) and public service announcements; information about resources available to help personnel and their families falls within this scope.

Figure 5.5. How Air Force Personnel Would Like to Receive Information About Resources Available to Help Them

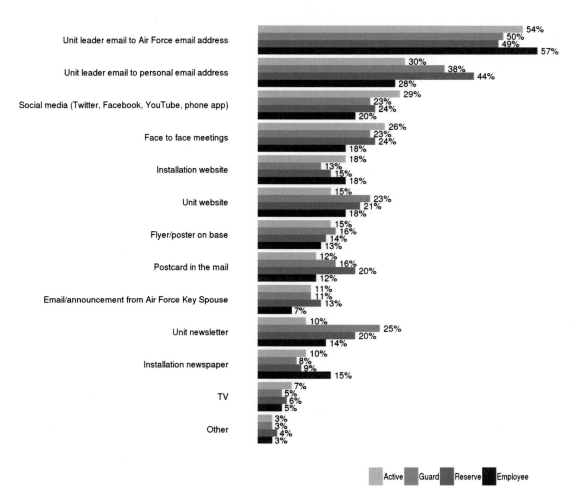

NOTE: *N* = 81,833 personnel. Responses from individuals who are both airmen and employees are included in both subgroups' results.

Figure 5.6 shows that 50% of spouses would appreciate learning about military resources via a mailed postcard. One way the 2017 Air Force Community Feedback Tool was promoted was through a postcard mailed to spouses, so it is possible that spouses participating in the survey were more likely to respond favorably to a postcard than those who did not participate. While it may be cost prohibitive to use postcards for routine communication or the entire spouse population, there may be certain vulnerable populations or particular events (e.g., on-base health fair or large-scale family event) for which this channel may be worthwhile to consider. Additionally, email and social media were popular choices. Among the least commonly preferred means of communication were flyers or posters on base, installation newspapers, and television announcements, which may reflect the relatively low percentage of spouse respondents who live on base (which is 20%).[34]

Figure 5.6. How Spouses Would Like to Receive Information About Resources Available to Help Them

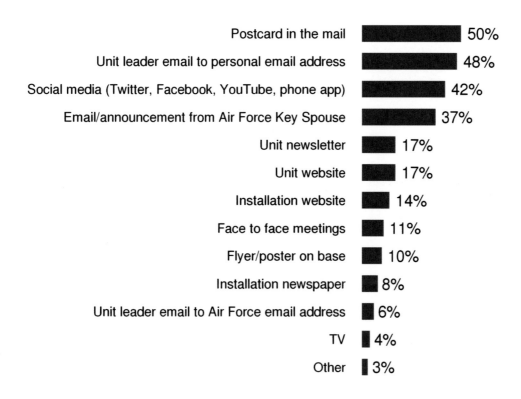

NOTES: *N* = 7,434 spouses. Spouses with Air Force email addresses would be those who are also civilian employees.

Exploring Variation in Responses: Discomfort Using or Difficulty Finding Out About Military Resources

Our choice of demographic and service history characteristics was guided by both practical and theoretical considerations, as described in Chapter 1. In general, we used similar sets of relevant characteristics for each model, with some modifications pertinent to each population, as described in Table 1.3. However, the models examined here inherently examine the process of seeking to address one's problems and needs; we therefore did not include the set of variables describing problem-solving status.

The item selected in this chapter for further exploration is whether the respondent indicated discomfort using military resources or difficulty finding out about them. To tap this item, we

---

[34] For more information, see appendix Table C.3.

created an index from several items developed for this survey gauging agreement on a 5-point scale ranging from 1 (strongly agree) to 5 (strongly disagree). As a reminder, the full item text was

- It is easy to find out about military resources for airmen and their families (asked only of airmen and spouses).
- When I have a problem finding the right military resource for my needs, I know who to contact to find help.
- If military resources are not meeting my needs, I know who to contact.
- I am comfortable using military resources available to me.

Because the first item was not asked of civilian employees who are not also airmen or spouses of airmen, that item was considered "missing" for that subgroup, but their responses to the other items were included.

This logic behind including this set of items for further examination is a practical one: The Air Force invests in resources to assist community members with problem-solving, well-being, and quality of life. Community members' level of comfort and familiarity with how to access military resources are important parts of help-seeking behavior. Community members who are not comfortable reaching out to military resources or who cannot find the appropriate ones for their situation cannot benefit, regardless of how well the programs and services are designed, are resourced, or use evidence-based approaches.

The index was constructed as an average across items (not a sum), meaning that the scale score was on the same 1-to-5 scale as individual items.[35] We judged differences of 0.25 point or more to be meaningful given the scale rather than reporting every statistically significant difference, no matter how small, or not reporting any at all. A 0.25 distinction on the 5-point scale could represent the difference between a neutral score and moving toward agreement with statements describing comfort with or ease of finding resources or from, on average, merely disagreeing with those statements to strongly disagreeing.[36]

Airmen

Although many characteristics achieved statistical significance in the model, only hours worked was both significant and reached the magnitude of potentially representing movement on the scale. Compared with airmen who worked less than 40 hours per week on average,

- Airmen who reported working 50 or more hours per week reported *greater* discomfort using or difficulty finding out about military resources.

---

[35] Weighted alphas for the index were acceptable: 0.89 among personnel.

[36] For technical readers, output with full model results is available from the authors.

Spouses of Airmen

Only two characteristics were both significant and sizable for spouses: rank of their airmen and home distance from base. Controlling for other characteristics in the model,

- Spouses married to junior enlisted airmen reported *greater* discomfort using or difficulty finding out about military resources than did spouses of officers and senior NCOs, as did spouses in our "airmen's rank unknown" category (note that these spouses were all themselves Air Force civilians).
- Spouses who lived more than 30 minutes away from base were more likely to report *greater* discomfort using or difficulty finding out about military resources than did spouses living on base.

Civilian Employees

Although several characteristics achieved statistical significance in the model, only two characteristics were both significant and sizable for Air Force civilian employees and both were related to military service: being dual-hatted (employees currently also serving as airmen), and being a military veteran. Controlling for other characteristics in the model,

- Dual-hatted airmen reported *less* discomfort using or difficulty finding out about military resources than did civilian employees who are not also guard or reserve airmen.
- Military veterans reported *less* discomfort using or difficulty finding out about military resources than did civilian employees who are not military veterans.

Findings and Conclusions

We asked all Air Force community members for general impressions of resources, whether they had reached out to them or not. Roughly 50% of surveyed personnel believed that each of the following has a good reputation: the chain of command, Airman (or Military) and Family Readiness Centers, chaplains or other members of military religious or spiritual groups, and support services for victims of violence. About 30% of Air Force personnel reported that the following have a good reputation: Child and Youth Programs; military hotline or referral line (such as Military OneSource or Military Crisis Line); military internet resources or social media; and, among married airmen, the Air Force Key Spouse Program. These were among the resources least likely to be perceived as having a good reputation. However, in some cases, such as Child and Youth Programs, many reported knowing little to nothing about them, which could mean that not everyone knows enough about these resources to know whether their reputation is good. Eligibility for some of the programs and resources varies, which can also influence familiarity. Among spouses, there was generally less agreement that military resources have a good reputation and more expressions of unfamiliarity with resources.

Other, more commonly applicable resources show a different pattern: Relatively few personnel reported that they knew little to nothing about their chain of command (11%); medical or health care provider (14%); or on-base Force Support Squadron resources, such as those for food and dining, fitness, lodging, and entertainment (19%). Asked to rate whether using any of these resources might hurt their (or their spouse or partner's) reputation, fewer than 5% felt that way for all resources but two: 11% thought there might be reputational consequences for seeing a mental health care provider, and 13% thought it might be harmful to contact the chain of command for help with problems or life challenges.

The majority of personnel agreed that it is easy to find out about military resources for airmen and their families (75%), that they know who to contact to find the right military resources (68%), and that they are comfortable using the military resources available to them (65%). In contrast, only 48% of spouses felt it is easy to find out about military resources, 41% know who to contact if they have a problem finding the right military resource for their needs, and 50% are comfortable using the military resources available to them. Additionally, 58% of personnel and 34% of spouses reported knowing who to contact if military resources are not meeting their needs.

Looking across the community populations examined, relatively few characteristics were related to comfort with or ease of finding out about the right military resources. For airmen, working 50 or more hours a week was related to greater discomfort or difficulty; for spouses, being married to junior enlisted airmen and living farther from base were related to greater discomfort or difficulty; and for civilians, those who were not also military veterans or current airmen felt greater discomfort or difficulty finding out about military resources. Taken together, these findings suggest that spouses, junior airmen, those with higher workloads, and civilian employees who have not served in the military need more guidance on the resources available to them and how to navigate the Air Force support system.

Email was the most commonly preferred method of receiving information from the Air Force about resources available to help them meet their needs: About 50% of personnel and spouses chose email as their preferred communication channel. Also, 50% of spouses expressed a preference for receiving information via postcard. Similar proportions of personnel preferred social media (20 to 29%) or face-to-face meetings (18% to 26%), and 42% of spouses indicated a preference for outreach via social media. Installation newspapers and television announcements were among the least commonly preferred ways of receiving information about support services.

Also note the lack of differences among populations that could theoretically be at greater risk for falling through the cracks. On this survey, Air Force personnel and spouses whose servicing installations were not led by the Air Force (such as joint bases managed by the Army or Navy) and Air Force personnel whose duty station was somewhere other than a military installation (e.g., a recruiting station, Reserve Officer Training Corps [ROTC] unit, or other government agency) did not report notable levels of greater discomfort using or difficulty finding out about military resources compared with the more typical situation of airmen working on an installation and one that is led by the Air Force. Additionally, personnel and the spouses of airmen assigned to remote and isolated locations and/or installations in a foreign country did not differ sizably from their counterparts who were in more highly populated areas and/or stateside in terms of average ratings of comfort with and ease of finding military resources. Because our findings cannot be taken as conclusive proof that location characteristics are not relevant, additional research should investigate these issues further. Taken together with findings regarding greater ease and comfort among community members who have multiple connections with the Air Force, however, these findings might suggest that, once familiarity with navigating the system is gained, it is transferrable to new situations.

6. Attitudes Toward the Military

The 2017 Air Force Community Feedback Tool also collected information about attitudes toward the military more generally. Satisfaction with the military and intentions to remain in the military are not only indicators of attitudes at the time of the survey but may also signal future behavior. This chapter addresses the following questions:

- What were community attitudes toward military service or employment?
- How satisfied were community members with aspects of military life?

Air Force Personnel Attitudes Toward Continuing Military Service or Employment

Air Force personnel rated their attitude toward continuing military service or employment on a 5-point scale with responses ranging from strongly favoring leaving at the next opportunity to strongly favoring staying.[37] Among the Air Force personnel who were not already separating or retiring soon, 64% of airmen favor staying in the military, and 76% of civilian employees favor continuing to work for the military. Figure 6.1 shows further details on these attitudes.

---

[37] For airmen, this question was worded this way: "Do you favor staying in the military or leaving at the next opportunity?" For employees, it read this way: "Do you favor continuing to work for the military or leaving at the next opportunity?"

Figure 6.1. Air Force Personnel's Attitudes About Leaving or Staying in Military Service or Employment

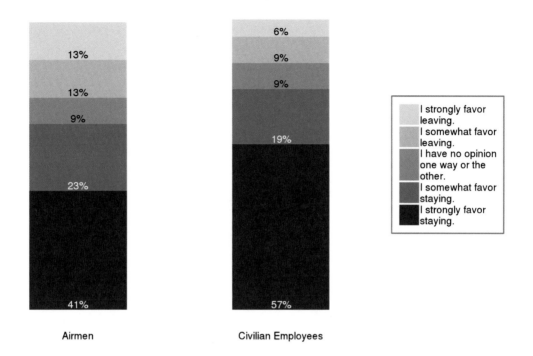

Airmen   Civilian Employees

NOTES: *N* = 46,218 airmen and 22,834 civilian employees. Responses from individuals who are both airmen and employees are included in both subgroups' results. Personnel who responded that this question was not applicable because they were already going to be separating or retiring soon are not included in this figure.

Personnel Beliefs About Their Spouse's or Partner's Support for Continuing Military Service or Employment

Air Force personnel who were married or in a committed romantic relationship were also asked to rate their perceptions of their spouses' or partners' attitudes toward their continuing military service or employment on a 5-point scale (strongly favor leaving to strongly favor staying), with an option to indicate that they did not know. These responses are shown in Figure 6.2. As with personnel's own attitudes about military service or employment, perceived support for continuing to serve was greater than perceived opposition. Among airmen, 56% believed their spouses or partners either strongly or somewhat favored their continuing to serve; among civilian employees, 66% believed their spouses or partners favored their continuing to work for the military.

91

Figure 6.2. Air Force Personnel's Perceptions of Their Spouses' or Partners' Attitudes Toward Their Military Service or Employment

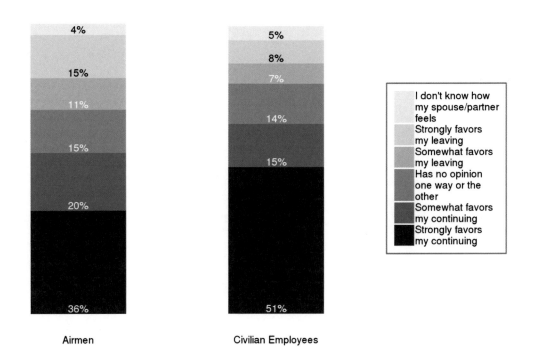

NOTES: *N* = 39,986 airmen and 20,290 civilian employees. Responses from individuals who are both airmen and employees are included in both subgroups' results.

Spouse's Attitudes Toward Their Airmen's Continuing Military Service

Mirroring the question for airmen about continued military service, spouses were asked whether they favored their airmen staying in the military or leaving at the next opportunity on a 5-point scale. Figure 6.3 shows the responses for spouses, excluding those who indicated that this question was not applicable because their airmen would be separating or retiring soon.

Figure 6.3. Spouse's Attitudes Toward Their Airmen Leaving or Staying in the Air Force (%)

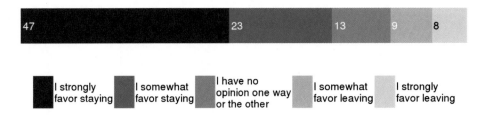

NOTES: *N* = 6,275 spouses. Responses from spouses who indicated that their airmen would soon be separating or retiring are not included in the figure.

92

Satisfaction with Military Life or Employment

Three items measured satisfaction with the military based on a 5-point scale ranging from very dissatisfied to very satisfied. Figure 6.4 displays responses to the question posed to airmen as: "Overall, how satisfied are you with the military way of life?" The wording for civilian employees was: "Overall, how satisfied are you with your military employment?" Taken as a whole, 69% of airmen and 78% of civilian employees in the overall Air Force were satisfied or very satisfied.

Figure 6.4. Air Force Personnel's Satisfaction with the Military Way of Life or Military Employment

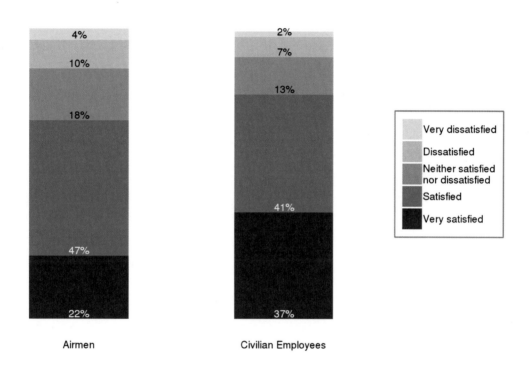

NOTES: *N* = 49,983 airmen and 22,904 civilian employees from the Air Force. Responses from individuals who are both airmen and employees are included in both subgroups' results.

Asked the same question as airmen about the military way of life, and using the same scale (ranging from very dissatisfied to very satisfied), 69% of spouses were satisfied or very satisfied with the military way of life (see Figure 6.5).

Figure 6.5. Spouses' Satisfaction with the Military Way of Life

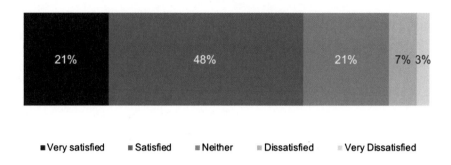

■ Very satisfied ■ Satisfied ■ Neither ■ Dissatisfied ▪ Very Dissatisfied

NOTE: *N* = 6,774 spouses.

Airman and Spouse Satisfaction with How the Air Force Treats Them and Their Families

All airmen were also asked how satisfied they were with the support and concern that the Air Force has for them and their families and the respect that the Air Force shows family members. Figure 6.6 shows that 71% of airmen were satisfied or very satisfied with the respect that the Air Force shows family members, and 63% were satisfied or very satisfied with the support and concern that the Air Force has for them and their families. On the negative end of the spectrum, 9% of airmen were dissatisfied or very dissatisfied with the respect shown to family members, and 15% were dissatisfied or very dissatisfied with Air Force support and concern for airmen and their families.[38]

---

[38] Civilian employees were not asked the items in this section because the Air Force has less direct involvement with civilian employee family life.

94

Figure 6.6. Airmen's Satisfaction with Air Force Respect, Support, and Concern for Them and Their Families

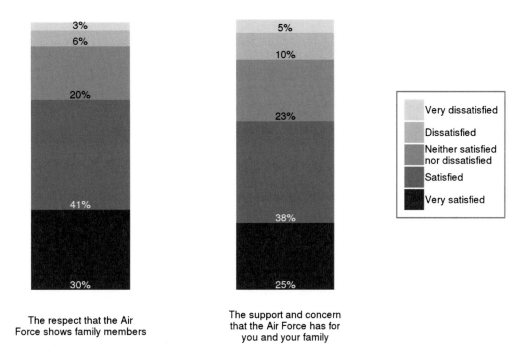

The respect that the Air Force shows family members

The support and concern that the Air Force has for you and your family

NOTE: *N* = 49,917 airmen.

Spouses of airmen were shown these same two items. Figure 6.7 shows that 67% were satisfied or very satisfied with the respect that Air Force shows family members, and 54% were satisfied or very satisfied with the support and concern that the Air Force has for them and their family. On the negative end of the spectrum, 11% of spouses were dissatisfied or very dissatisfied with the respect the Air Force shows family members, and 16% were dissatisfied or very dissatisfied with the support and concern for airmen and their families.

Figure 6.7. Spouse Satisfaction with Air Force Respect, Support, and Concern for Them and Their Families (%)

The respect that the Air Force shows family members

The support and concern that the Air Force has for you and your family

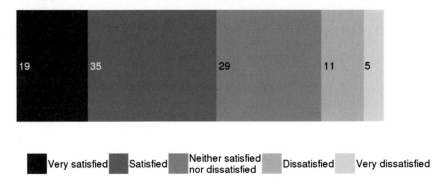

NOTES: *N* = 6,769 spouses.

Exploring Variation in Responses: Satisfaction and Preference for Military Service or Employment

Our choice of demographic and service history characteristics was guided by both practical and theoretical considerations as described in Chapter 1. In general, we used similar sets of relevant characteristics for each model, with some modifications pertinent to each population, as described in Table 1.3. As described in Chapter 1, we also included a set of variables describing problem-solving status.

We included two types of measures related to attitudes toward the military in our modeling: a single item measuring attitudes toward military service and a composite index measuring satisfaction with military life and how the Air Force treats its families.[39] All items for these two measures used a corresponding continuum of values ranging from 1 to 5, and we judged statistically significant differences of 0.25 point or more to be meaningful. Such a difference could represent moving from neutral to somewhat likely to favor staying in the military or being somewhat satisfied with military life and how the Air Force treats military families, or from

---

[39] For technical readers, output with full model results is available from the authors.

merely somewhat favoring to strongly favoring leaving service or employment, for example. The following describes these measures:

- **Attitudes toward military service or employment.** The first item for further exploration is whether respondents who were not already separating or retiring soon favor or strongly favor staying or leaving military service or employment. For spouses, we were able to examine the spouse equivalent, which assessed whether or not they favored their airmen staying in the military. This outcome is relevant because it is a well-known and powerful predictor of actual attrition (Hom and Griffeth, 1995; Griffeth, Hom, and Gaertner, 2000). Spousal support of retention has also been demonstrated as a key factor affecting actual military retention (e.g., Burnam, et al., 1992; Campbell, Luchman, and Kuhn, 2017; Segal and Harris, 1993). For example, one recent study analyzing spouse responses to the 2012 Survey of Active Duty Spouses linked to military administrative files on service members' active duty status and separation and enlistment status found that spousal support was a significant predictor of service members' actual retention two years after the survey (Campbell, Luchman, and Kuhn, 2017). Particularly relevant for this report, the analyses showed that, "Air Force members whose spouses strongly favored them staying on active duty stayed at a rate of about 19 for every 1 who left compared to Air Force members whose spouses strongly favored them leaving, who stayed at a rate of 3 for every 2 who left" (Campbell, Luchman, and Kuhn, 2017, p. 4).
- **Airman and spouse satisfaction with military life and how the Air Force treats military families.** We also used a brief composite index of three items asked only of airmen and spouses of airmen. These items assess both satisfaction with "the military way of life" and satisfaction with how the Air Force treats family members. These are sometimes considered as separate constructs: Satisfaction with the military way of life has been analyzed as a single item (as in Booth, Segal, and Bell, 2007) or as part of a construct of external adaptation toward the military (as in Pittman, Kerpelman, and McFadyen, 2004). Taken together, these items can be seen as addressing overall perceptions of family life in the military. These attitudes are important because they influence such factors as spouse support for retention. In combining the items, we took the average so that we could describe results in terms of the 5-point Likert scale, ranging from very dissatisfied to very satisfied, used for the individual items.[40]

Airmen

Several military service and demographic characteristics we considered were associated with these attitudinal variables, but none of the location characteristics met our criteria for statistical significance and magnitude of change in average ratings. For reference, overall, the average score for airmen regarding their preference to remain in the military was 3.7, which falls between neutral and somewhat favoring staying. The overall satisfaction score was 3.8, which falls between the neutral rating (3) and satisfied (4). Table 6.1 gives an overview of airman characteristics.

---

[40] Alpha for these three items was acceptable at 0.86.

Table 6.1. Overview of Characteristics Associated With Notable Differences in Airmen's Satisfaction and Preference to Remain in the Military

		Preference to Remain in the Military	Satisfaction with Military Life/ Treatment of Families
Location	U.S. or foreign		
	Remote and isolated		
	Non–Air Force–led installation		
	Somewhere other than an installation		
Military service	Component	✓	✓
	Rank group	✓	
	Military career group	✓	
	Distance from base		
	Personnel nights away from home		
	Personnel hours working Air Force duties		✓
Demographic	Marital status		
	Minor child(ren)		
Problem-solving status		✓	✓

As was true for many of the regression models for airmen, component was relevant to both turnover intentions and satisfaction with military life and/or treatment of families. Controlling for all other characteristics included in the models,

- Compared with active component airmen, guard and reserve were more likely, by about 0.50 point on average, to favor staying in the military and had about 0.25-point higher satisfaction rating.

As it was in other models, rank group was also relevant here:

- In comparison with junior enlisted airmen, all other rank groups reported a *greater* average preference to remain in the military by at least 0.25 point.

Relevant characteristics also included career group. Compared with being in the operations career group (the reference group), the following two groups were each associated with a *greater* average preference to remain in the military, by about 0.25 point:

- the acquisition career group

- an occupational category that combines the smaller professional career group (legal and chaplain), special investigations career group, and airmen holding special duty identifiers (e.g., recruiters, first sergeants, instructors, honor guard).[41]

Working 50 or more hours a week was associated with about 0.25-point *lower* satisfaction rating than working less than 40.

Problem-solving status was significantly associated with both items. Compared with airmen whose needs for their top problem in the past year went unmet despite reaching out for help, the following airmen all had a *greater* preference to remain in the military and a *higher* satisfaction rating:

- airmen who did not have a problem at all in the past year
- airmen who had no perceived need for help with their top problem
- airmen who did not contact resources for help with their top problem because their problems were otherwise resolved
- airmen who reached out for help with their top problem and had their needs met.

Compared with having unmet needs, each group was associated with between 0.25-point and over 0.50-point improvement on satisfaction and a similar reduction in turnover intentions (preference to leave the military). Not having a problem at all was associated with the largest reduction.

Spouses of Airmen

Overall, the average score for spouses' preferences regarding their airmen staying in the military was 3.9, which falls between neutral and favoring staying. The overall satisfaction score was 3.7, which falls between the neutral rating and satisfied with military life and Air Force treatment of families. Table 6.2 gives an overview of spouse characteristics. We also examined relevant associations for spouses of airmen. Location characteristics did not meet our criteria. While several of the demographic and military service characteristics were statistically significant, the differences were in general somewhat small—with the exception of problem-solving status. Notably,

- Both guard and reserve spouses' preferences for their airmen to stay in the military were, on average, about 0.25 point lower than those of spouses of active component members.
- Spouses of junior NCOs were, on average, 0.25 point more likely to favor staying than were spouses of junior enlisted.
- Spouses who live 30 minutes or more from base were just under 0.25 point more likely to favor their airman leaving and also less satisfied.

---

[41] As noted earlier, this category includes several enlisted occupations or positions not available to new airmen, so this finding could reflect a greater concentration in this group of airmen who are on average further along in their careers and have already decided to stay until retirement, if possible.

Table 6.2. Overview of Characteristics Associated with Notable Differences in Spouses' Satisfaction and Support for Their Airmen to Remain in the Military

		Support to Remain in the Military	Satisfaction with Military Life/ Treatment of Families
Location	U.S. or foreign		
	Remote and isolated		
	Non–Air Force–led installation		
	Somewhere other than an installation		
Military service [a]	Component	✓	
	Rank group[b]	✓	
	Distance from base	✓	✓
	Personnel nights away from home		
	Personnel hours working Air Force duties		
Demographic	Spouse employment		
	Minor child(ren)		
Problem-solving status		✓	✓

[a] In the spouse models, component, rank group, nights away from home and hours working refer to their airmen's characteristics.
[b] Not asked of spouses who are also civilian employees.

For both attitudes toward their airmen's military service and satisfaction with military life and treatment of families, we included problem-solving status in the model. This status was statistically significantly associated with both items. As might be expected, compared with spouses whose needs for their top problem went unmet despite reaching out for help,

- Not having a problem at all was associated with a *greater* preference to remain in the military by almost 0.50 point and an increase in satisfaction by almost 1 point.
- Spouses that reported not needing help for their top problem were *more* likely to support staying in the military (the difference was between 0.25 and 0.50 point), had *higher* satisfaction (by about 0.50 point).
- Those who reached out for help and whose needs were met for their top problem were also more likely to prefer staying in the military by about 0.33 point, and their satisfaction was higher by about 0.50 point. Those who did not contact resources because their top problems were otherwise resolved and those who did not reach out for help with their greatest needs for some other reason also had *higher* satisfaction (by 0.50 and 0.25 point, respectively).

Civilian Employees

For civilians, the one item we examined in greater depth was whether they favored continuing to work for the military or leaving at the next opportunity. The average rating on this scale of 1 to 5 was 4.11, which falls between somewhat favoring and strongly favoring continuing their military employment. None of the location, military service, or demographic characteristics we examined were associated with this preference to a degree that met our criteria of statistical significance and magnitude. Problem-solving status, however, was significantly associated with intentions to leave. Compared with having unmet needs for the top past-year problem—despite reaching out for help,

- Not having a problem at all in the past year was associated with a *greater* preference for continuing to work for the military by about 1 point.
- Having problems but perceiving no corresponding need for assistance with the top problem was associated with a *greater* preference for staying by about 0.50 point.
- Having the greatest needs for their top problem resolved (either by using or not using resources) was associated with a *greater* preference for staying by between 0.50 point and one point.
- Not reaching out for help with their top problem for some reason other than that the problem was resolved (i.e., belief there is nothing anyone can do, did not want to ask for help, did not know who to contact) was associated with a *greater* preference for staying by just over 0.25 point.

Findings and Conclusions

Among personnel not separating or retiring soon, the majority favored continuing their service or employment. When we asked airmen and civilian employees about their spouses' or partners' support for continued connection to the Air Force, perceived support for continuing to serve was greater than perceived opposition. We also asked spouses their preferences directly, and a majority did report that they strongly or somewhat supported the continued military service of their airman spouse.

We also asked items tapping satisfaction with various aspects of connection to the military: Airmen were asked about satisfaction with the military way of life, while civilian employees were asked about their satisfaction with military employment. In both cases, majorities reported being satisfied or very satisfied. Airmen and spouses were also queried regarding Air Force treatment of families. In general, both airmen and spouses were satisfied with the respect the Air Force shows family members, although perceptions of support and concern were somewhat less positive.

We further explored attitudes toward continuing military service or employment and, for airmen and spouses, developed a three-item index tapping satisfaction with military life and how the Air Force treats military families. A variety of characteristics were associated with increased airmen preference to leave military service, including being in the active component (compared with being in the reserve component), and being junior enlisted (compared with all other rank groups). For their spouses, living farther away from base, being an active component spouse (compared with being the spouse of an airman in the reserve component), and being the spouse

101

of a junior enlisted airman were all associated with an increase in support for leaving the military at the next opportunity. For airmen, spouses of airmen, and civilian employees, those whose greatest needs for their top problem went unmet despite reaching out for assistance had a higher preference for leaving than did those whose needs were met.

Turning to satisfaction, for airmen, working 50 or more hours a week (rather than less than 40) was associated with a decrease in satisfaction with military life or treatment of families, as was being in the active component. For spouses, being farther from base (30 minutes or more) was associated with a decrease in satisfaction. For both airmen and their spouses, successful resolution of their top problem was associated with higher satisfaction than was having unmet needs.

Controlling for all other factors in the models, we did not find evidence to support the idea that family factors—marital status or minor children—were associated with either satisfaction or desire to leave the military. This finding does not necessarily mean that military life has no substantial impact on Air Force families or that family factors do not play a role in airmen's attitudes or preferences. It may be that the benefits of military life and the various support programs and services help mitigate the downsides of service for families; further research would be needed before firm conclusions could be drawn that family factors play no role whatsoever in airman satisfaction or desire to leave the military.

Taken together, these findings reinforce the vulnerability of particular groups (active component airmen, junior enlisted, airmen who bear a heavy workload, and those that live farther away from Air Force resources) and highlight the positive effects that being able to successfully solve life's problems can have on all members of the Air Force community.

7. Correlations Between Key Indicators of Interest

In Chapters 2 through 6, we presented descriptive results for a number of survey items and selected a few key indicators of interest for greater exploration. As noted previously, while many community member attitudes and experiences are potentially of interest, in general we prioritized the items most likely to be important from a policy perspective, those that had proven useful in prior research, or those of particular interest to the Air Force. The selected indicators of interest included

- limited-activity days in the past month that are due to poor physical or mental health
- perceived resilience
- discomfort using or difficulty finding out about military resources
- satisfaction with military life and how the Air Force treats airmen and their families
- unmet needs associated with the top type of past-year problems, despite individuals having reached out for assistance
- preference to leave military service or employment (turnover intentions).

Through statistical models, we explored whether community members' responses varied by location, military service, and demographic characteristics. When appropriate, we also explored whether they varied by problem-solving status.

Military service characteristics have the potential to be relevant for community attitudes and experiences because they can represent tenure and position within the hierarchy, level of familiarity and interaction with the Air Force, work environment (e.g., because it may differ by career group), and the degree to which the demands of Air Force duties may compete with time for friends, family, or self-care. Marital status, having minor children, and employment status among spouses are also characteristics that could influence individuals' perceptions of their well-being, the types of the problems they might experience, their ability to meet their and their families' needs, and their satisfaction with military life or employment.

The primary focus of these analyses was on the variables that could guide outreach and program planning purposes: Air Force leaders may wish to know which types of locations and which demographic subgroups may have greater or different types of needs so that leaders and providers can tailor initiatives appropriately. Overall, there were, indeed, a number of ways that community members' responses to these selected indicators of interest were associated with military service or demographic characteristics, and these differences rose to a level of magnitude or statistical significance that the observed location characteristics generally did not.

This chapter further explores these key concepts to provide an understanding of whether there were relationships between these variables of interest in the responses from airmen, civilian employees and spouses of airmen. We conducted analyses that would allow us to understand whether responses to one question or set of questions were associated with responses to other questions. We report simple bivariate correlations between these constructs to shed light on which variables were more strongly related.

Table 7.1, for Air Force personnel, and Table 7.2, for spouses, present correlations between the various attitudinal outcomes and other indicators, along with our measure of unmet needs. Given our large sample sizes, it is not surprising that all correlations in the tables are statistically significant (different from zero, or no relationship; $p <0.001$). Positive numbers represent a positive relationship between the key indicators of interest (higher values on one item or scale tend to be associated with higher values on the other), while negative numbers represent an inverse relationship. The closer the value is to 1 or -1, the stronger the relationship: Using a widely adopted benchmark, a relationship may be considered strong if it is <-0.5 or >0.5 (highlighted in blue), moderate if it is between -0.3 and -0.5 or between 0.3 and 0.5 (highlighted in the paler blue), and weak if it is between -0.1 and -0.3 or between 0.1 and 0.3 (not highlighted) (Cohen, 1988). This type of analysis can reveal only whether there is an association between indicators of interest, not whether one *causes* the other. It also does not control for other characteristics or variables that could help further explain the relationships between key indicators of interest because that was beyond the scope of this effort.

Table 7.1. Interrelationships Between Air Force Personnel's Responses to Key Indicators of Interest

	Limited-Activity Days Due to Poor Health	Perceived Resilience	Discomfort Using or Difficulty Finding Out About Military Resources	Satisfaction with Military Life/ Treatment of Families[a]	Unmet Needs
Limited-activity days that are due to poor health	1.00				
Perceived resilience	−0.24	1.00			
Discomfort using or difficulty finding out about military resources	0.20	−0.32	1		
Satisfaction with the military[a]	−0.25	0.33	−0.52	1.00	
Unmet needs	0.14	−0.11	0.32	−0.33	1.00
Airman turnover intentions[b]	0.20	−0.26	0.28	−0.57	0.21
Employee turnover intentions[c]	0.16	−0.22	0.32	Not applicable	0.25

[a] Items presented only to airmen and their spouses.
[b] Version of the item presented only to airmen
[c] Version of the item presented only to Air Force civilians.

Table 7.2. Interrelationships Between Spouses' Responses to Key Indicators of Interest

	Limited-Activity Days Due to Poor Health	Perceived Resilience	Discomfort Using or Difficulty Finding Out About Military Resources	Satisfaction with the Military	Unmet Needs
Limited-activity days that are due to poor health	1.00				
Perceived resilience	−0.26	1.00			
Discomfort using or difficulty finding out about military resources	0.13	−0.26	1.00		
Satisfaction with the military	−0.17	0.26	−0.51	1.00	
Unmet needs	0.14	−0.13	0.27	−0.31	1.00
Spouse turnover intentions	0.06	−0.19	0.19	−0.50	0.14

Although some of these correlations are small in magnitude, all are in the expected direction. Furthermore, correlations that are larger in magnitude tend to be those with "source" similarity: That is, both are related to the military. For example, discomfort with using *military* resources was more strongly related to satisfaction with the *military* than it was to perceived resilience.

For both Air Force personnel and spouses, the number of limited-activity days that are due to poor mental or physical health was only weakly associated with the other indicators of interest, including perceived resilience.

For Air Force personnel, greater perceived resilience was moderately associated with a lower level of discomfort using or difficulty finding out about military resources. For spouses of airmen, the same relationship was only a weak association. For personnel, having unmet needs among those who reached out for assistance was moderately associated with a level of discomfort using or difficulty finding out about military resources, but that relationship among spouses was again weak. However, the relationships here suggest that increasing comfort with resources has the potential to decrease unmet needs.

The strongest relationships detected revolved around airmen's and spouses' satisfaction with military life and treatment of families. Recall that the measure includes satisfaction with the military way of life, the respect the Air Force shows family members, and the support and concern the Air Force has for them as airmen or spouses and their families. For both airmen and spouses, the measure of discomfort with using military resources or difficulty finding out about them was relatively strongly associated with lower satisfaction with military life or treatment of families (as noted above, both variables also have in common their direct connection with aspects of the military organization itself). Moderately associated with satisfaction were (a) airmen's perceptions of their own resilience and (b) airmen and spouses' sense of whether their needs for their top past-year problem were met after having reached out to military and/or nonmilitary resources for assistance.

Moreover, this measure of satisfaction with military life and treatment of families was strongly related to turnover intentions, both of airmen themselves and spouses' attitudes toward their airmen's continued military service. As one would expect, lower satisfaction was associated with greater preference for leaving the military. This finding suggests that interventions that target one of these related variables may have second-order effects on other variables that were strongly related. Although the strength of the relationships may be attenuated or exacerbated over the passage of time during the problem-solving process, targeting interventions at earlier points in the process, such as increasing comfort with or access to information about military resources, may be beneficial downstream.

Civilian employees' discomfort using or difficulty finding out about military resources was moderately associated with their turnover intentions, so there may be a similar need for improving employees' ability to learn about what types of assistance they are eligible for that could help meet their needs.

8. Key Findings, Conclusions, and Recommendations

The 2017 Air Force Community Feedback Tool provided a self-reported needs assessment of active, guard, and reserve airmen; their spouses; and Air Force civilian employees. It also provided feedback on the use of military and nonmilitary resources, as well as overall indicators of interest to the Air Force. It represents a new approach for examining these issues within the Air Force. The ultimate purpose of this assessment was to inform CAB Community Action Plans for installations, MAJCOMs and equivalents, the Air National Guard, and the overall Air Force. Previously, tailored descriptive reports were provided to the locations and organizations listed in Appendix A. The first priority of this survey effort was to provide actionable feedback to these leaders and service providers. The second priority of this effort was to provide an overview of these indicators across the Air Force and to explore ways community members' attitudes or experiences may have varied by type of location, demographic, or military service characteristics and thereby highlight places or demographic subgroups that may need additional outreach or revision of existing programs, policies, or services to meet their needs. It was not possible within the scope of this effort to explore all possible variations by subgroup or to pursue all other analyses of interest, so we prioritized topics or individual characteristics of particular concern to the sponsor or community leaders or hypothesized to hold particular relevance in previous research. From some of the key findings from our analyses, we derived several conclusions.

Key Findings and Conclusions

Three Problems Were Most Frequently Rated as Sole or Most Significant

Although about 10% of Air Force personnel and 8% of spouses reported experiencing no problems in the past year, most community members did report facing challenges. Community members indicated that their top problems were related to military practices and culture, work-life balance, and their own well-being. Specific issues that stood out across these three types as having the potential to relate to work-life conflict were perceptions of poor leadership, challenges managing competing commitments, finding enough time for self-care, and problems with sleep and stress. These results are remarkably similar to those provided by active duty Army soldiers who participated in a 2014 Army-specific survey employing a similar survey framework. In that survey, 40% of soldiers said their top issues were one or more of the following: feeling stressed, overwhelmed, or tired; trouble sleeping; and poor communication with coworkers or superiors (Sims et al., 2017, p. xiii). Indeed, these problems are not unique to the Air Force or even DoD.

Of the three most common top problems in the Air Force survey, personnel whose top problems concerned military practices and culture were more likely to rate their problems as "severe" at their worst (31%), compared with those who had problems with their own well-being (25% rated as severe) or work-life balance (20% rated as severe). Junior enlisted and NCOs were more likely to choose financial and legal problems and military practices and culture problems than were other rank groups, potentially reflecting lower pay and/or lower position within the organization.

Some Did Not Need Help, But Those Who Did Had a Variety of Needs

Among community members who experienced problems in the past year, substantial minorities reported not needing assistance (40% of personnel and 33% of spouses). For those who did have a need, frequently chosen categories included advice, coaching, or education and general information (among personnel) and general information and emotional or social support (among spouses).

Overall, 58% of Air Force personnel with at least one problem in the past year who contacted someone for assistance reported that they had unmet needs, despite reaching out. The problem type for which the highest proportion of personnel indicated unmet needs was for military practices and culture, at 54%. The most frequent problem type for which spouses reported not having their needs met after reaching out was also military practices and culture.

Among personnel who had problems in the military practices and culture problem type, 18% expressed a need for general information, while 16% indicated a need for advice, coaching, or education. Among spouses dealing with military practices and culture problems, the most commonly selected needs were for specific information (26%) or general information (24%). Although offering information in a way that personnel and spouses can access, understand, and act on is an ongoing challenge, it is possible that some of the solutions to military practices and culture problems may be relatively straightforward. However, other needs may be related to the sometimes demanding nature of the work, for which solutions are less clear cut.

Those with Problems Who Did Reach Out Contacted a Range of Resources

Community members who reached out to military resources most often reported contacting the chain of command or other military coworkers or friends or military spouses, so having a chain of command and a community well-informed of available resources are essential. Of institutional sources of help outside the chain of command, mental and medical health care providers were sought by many, even though our findings in some cases highlighted some concerns regarding reaching out to these types of sources because of the potential to harm an airman's reputation (also a concern for some when going to the chain of command). Personnel and spouses who reached out to military mental health care providers or chaplains or other members of military religious or spiritual groups were among those most likely to indicate that such resources helped "a lot"; however, even for these top rated resources, fewer than 33% felt they helped "a lot." Moreover, about 20% of community members reported that their personal networks did not have the resources or ability to help them. It is important to note that not all community members who believed they needed help with their top type of problem reached out to military or nonmilitary resources for assistance. Indeed, about 10% did not reach out to any resources.

Unmet Needs Among Those Who Reached Out for Help May Require Leader Involvement

Among airmen who reached out for help with their problems, characteristics associated with unmet needs (of any type) include living 30 or more minutes away from base and spending 180 nights or more in a given year away from home because of military duties, such as deployments, temporary duty, training, and field exercises. In addition to nights away from home, other aspects of high workload can also be influential in whether or not personnel get their needs met: Both airmen and civilian employees who reported working 50 or more hours per week and the spouses of airmen who bear a similar workload were more likely to have had unmet needs. Combined with the influence of long work hours—and the military's role in managing workload and manpower—on a variety of relevant outcomes for airmen (top problem selection, unmet needs, days limited by poor health, and attitudes toward the Air Force), these suggest that Community Action Plans need input and buy-in from both the chain of command and service providers. Although those who reached out to helping professionals (such as behavioral health personnel and chaplains) noted that they were helpful in solving problems and must undoubtedly be part of the solution, this pattern of findings suggests that, without recourse to the military system itself, such intervention may be merely treating the symptoms. To address some of the issues the survey uncovered, leadership at all levels must be involved not only in planning resources but in considering interventions that would more generally be considered to be related to the workplace than to behavioral health. Our findings also speak more to broad issues than to local specifics, and local context and solutions will need to be assessed and incorporated into planning—as the Air Force is attempting to do.

Having problems that were resolved, rather than having unmet needs, was associated with improved outcomes on many of the items we selected for further examination. However, it appears that those who did not need help with their problems or did not reach out because the problem had been solved experienced better outcomes. Those who faced no problems fared still better. In some senses, this is similar to the phenomenon when individuals seek mental health care. Care may improve their outcomes and is essential to provide for this reason. But simply not having a mental health challenge at all, or facing a relatively minor challenge, is better still. Life is full of challenges, and the military cannot alleviate all challenges before they happen; the clear takeaway is that availability of resources to help solve problems is indeed a helpful benefit to the Air Force community. Even when resources are available, however, providing information about them is key.

Many Reported Discomfort Using or Difficulty Finding Out About Military Resources

The majority of personnel agreed that it was easy to find out about military resources for airmen and their families (75%), that they knew who to contact to find the right military resources (68%), and that they are comfortable using the available military resources (65%). In contrast, only 48% of spouses felt it was easy to find out about military resources, 41% knew who to contact if they had a problem finding the right military resource for their needs, and 50% were comfortable using military resources available to them. Additionally, 58% of personnel and 34% of spouses reported knowing who to contact if military resources are not meeting their needs.

We found that relatively few characteristics were related to a potentially meaningful change in level of comfort with or ease of finding the right military resources. For airmen, having a heavy workload was related to greater discomfort with or difficulty finding out about resources, which could be related to lack of time in the day to do so. For spouses, being married to junior enlisted airmen and living farther from base (where many resources are advertised or located) was related to greater discomfort or difficulty finding out about resources. Civilians who were not also military veterans or current airmen felt greater discomfort or difficulty finding military resources, which could be related to a relative lack of familiarity with (and eligibility for) the array of available resources because these individuals had less time with and exposure to the military overall.

Taken together, this suggests that the key is having the *opportunity* to become familiar with what is available. Spouses, in particular, may have difficulty finding out about what is available. Among guard spouses, 67% knew little to nothing about the guard's Family Assistance Center; among all spouses, 60% or more said they knew little to nothing about military hotlines or referral lines; resources for legal and policy violations; and support services for victims of violence, such as sexual assault or domestic violence. Moreover, 59% of spouses were unfamiliar with the Air Force Key Spouse Program; 55% were unfamiliar with Child and Youth Programs; 50% were unfamiliar with military chaplains or other members of military religious or spiritual groups and 52% were unfamiliar with military mental health care providers. Although there is a continuous stream of new spouses to orient to Air Force and other military resources, these results suggest there still may be room to make more spouses aware of the resources available to support them and their families.

Our findings suggested that interventions to alleviate discomfort and lack of familiarity with resources should target airmen whose workloads make learning what is available difficult and should include particular outreach to spouses of more junior airmen and spouses who live farther away. Civilians who lack familiarity with resources via other means, such as their own military service, should also be a focus of outreach.

Some Types of Problems Were Resolved and Some Characteristics Were Less Influential

The majority of personnel whose top problem types were their own well-being (which was one of the three most frequent top problem types) or household management indicated that their needs were met (59% and 58%, respectively). Similarly, a majority of spouses indicated that their needs were met when their top problem type was their own well-being or household management (63% and 58%, respectively). Although a numerical majority of personnel and spouses with needs were able to find resources to help them resolve these problems, the size of the minority that did not get needed help is still potentially a cause for concern.

Sleeping problems, fatigue, and stress were each reported by about 50% of personnel who selected their own well-being as their top type of past-year problem. Stress, fatigue, managing weight, and mood (e.g., depression, anger) were the issues most commonly reported by spouses for whom well-being was their top problem in the past year (61% reported stress, about 50% reported each of the other issues).

Regardless of top problem, out of a list of military resources, mental health care providers as well as religious or spiritual resources had the greatest percentages of respondents who reached out to them that felt that they helped "a lot." Yet only 31–32% of personnel and spouses indicated that military mental health care providers helped "a lot," while 17–18% of personnel and spouses reported the same for military medical or health care providers. Among those who turned to a private, medical provider not paid for by the military or a private, mental health care provider not paid for by the military, 32–34% of personnel and spouses felt these nonmilitary resources helped a lot with their needs.

In terms of overall indicators of well-being, more than 55% of community members believed that their health is excellent or very good, and only 1–2% rated it poor. On average, the number of self-reported poor physical health days in the past month was 3.9 among Air Force personnel and 3.3 among spouses of airmen. The average number of self-reported poor mental health days in the past month was 3.4 among Air Force personnel and 4.5 among spouses of airmen. Turning to the measure of perceived resilience, 2017 scores within the Air Force community were similar to scores found in the general population and varied very little across demographic subgroups. For a more detailed summary of specific health and well-being findings, see Appendix E.

Generally speaking, we did not find evidence for major differences in responses from community members in remote or isolated locations, serving in a foreign country, serving on a non–Air Force–led installation, or serving somewhere other than an installation (such as a recruiting station, an ROTC unit, with another agency). Although our findings do not represent proof that such characteristics are not relevant, they suggest that other characteristics are more influential for a variety of relevant indicators ranging from level of comfort with resources to unmet needs. Our findings in several areas highlight the benefits of experience with the system and resource availability—for example, those with more connections to the Air Force, such as veterans now serving as civilian employees and airmen and their spouses with more seniority, tended to have more comfort with resources. Less-junior personnel and those with spouses who work were also less likely to select such problems as financial and legal challenges as their top type of problem.

Leader Emails Were Preferred Ways of Learning About Resources

In terms of means of outreach, personnel preferences for unit leader emails to Air Force email addresses topped the list, followed by a preference for leaders to send emails to their personal email address. Unit leader emails to personal email addresses were also one of the top preferences among spouses. That preference for sending information to a personal email account makes particular sense for the guard and reserve members, who infrequently have access to their official Air Force email account (e.g., drill weekends), and for spouses, who do not have official Air Force email accounts. Not everyone may be comfortable providing their personal email address to their or their spouses' chain of command or wish to receive official Air Force communication through both their personal and official email address, but some clearly prefer it over other forms of communication. Installation newspapers and television announcements were among the least commonly preferred channels for receiving information about support services.

Implications

To summarize, when some of the key findings of the study are taken together, these findings reinforce the potential greater or differing needs of particular groups (active component airmen, junior enlisted and their spouses, personnel who bear a heavy workload, and airmen and spouses who live farther from Air Force resources) and highlight the importance to the Air Force community of being able to successfully solve life's problems. This work provides an Air Force–level overview of the Air Force Community Feedback Tool, which represents a new approach for examination of community needs and resilience for the Air Force. Although they are too technical for the body of the report, we offer suggestions for future administrations in Appendix B. In the following sections, we offer some considerations for additional data analysis that the Air Force may wish to pursue and finally, based on our findings, some suggestions and recommendations on how to respond to community feedback.

Recommendations for Further Data Analysis

As we did with community members' top type of problem in the past year, we recommend exploring further whether the perceived needs that correspond to those problems vary by location, demographic, or military service characteristics. It could be hypothesized that certain subgroups (e.g., junior enlisted airmen, guard or reserve airmen, community members who live 30 minutes or more from base, personnel who work somewhere other than a military installation) might have had a greater need for information than others or that certain subgroups would characterize their needs as being for advice, coaching, or education rather than professional counseling, which would have implications for how support is marketed and offered.

For any demographic subgroups the Air Force CAB decides to prioritize in terms of outreach, specific analyses could be run on how they would like to be contacted. Further exploration may also reveal subgroup differences in the individual issues within their top problem category. As noted earlier, we did not explore all possible military service or demographic characteristics captured by the survey, such as gender, race, ethnicity, education level, permanent change of station move in the previous 12 months. For guard members we did not examine whether there were differences between those serviced by a stand-alone guard wing and those serviced by an active or reserve installation. Future analyses to be conducted to delve more deeply into these aspects of the population and how they manage life's challenges.

Recommendations to Respond to Community Feedback

We offer the following specific recommendations for Air Force–level responses to this community feedback, although many could apply to local level efforts as well:

- Pay special attention to challenges associated with the top three most frequently reported types of problem that the community felt mattered most: military practices and culture, well-being, and work-life balance. Particularly for Air Force personnel, the reported frequencies of these top problem types clearly rise above others. Thus, initiatives targeted at resolving issues within these domains may be likely to serve the communities.

  - Some of the interventions needed may already be relatively straightforward and not require a change in policy or a new or revised program; for example, community members often thought their needs related to military practices and culture problems were for information or advice. In such situations, simply making sure these programs and services are accessible and known may be sufficient. However, some of the issues reported for this problem type, such as poor leadership, are potentially more difficult to manage and may need to be addressed through leadership training or professional military education.

- Promote creative peer-to-peer information-sharing about available resources. Examples could include self-made videos, Instagram challenges, poster design contests, Twitter chats, scavenger hunts (e.g., locating different resources or providers)—use popular but appropriate means of tapping into the creativity, energy, and social networks within the community. New approaches that engage user-generated social media content trends seem warranted given the lack of community awareness about many key resources, difficulty some community members reported finding out about resources, and the apparent tendency of so many community members to look to military coworkers, friends, and other military spouses for help with their needs. The Air Force can help facilitate brainstorming, enlisting volunteers, and providing the accurate and useful information to feed into the dissemination strategies.

- Consider improvements in Air Force management of workload. Some personnel problems, such as those related to work-life balance and military practices and culture, may reflect a need for better Air Force management of their workload. Where personnel are persistently stretched thin (e.g., often working 50 or more hours a week), strategies could include reducing requirements, increasing manpower, and seeking ways to reorganize or reallocate the work so it can be done more efficiently. Installation leaders may not have the authority or resources to implement some of these changes without support from higher levels of the organization. Additionally, leaders should be mindful that the workload may actually increase in the short term to implement changes that lead to long-term workload reductions. For example, existing personnel may need to take on additional duties to bring new personnel up to speed before some relief in workload occurs. To truly achieve the desired benefits of organizational changes to reduce workload, leadership and policymakers should be mindful of the short-term increased burden on already stressed units and, in the longer term, should resist the temptation to use new efficiencies gained to stretch the workload back to maximum capacity.

  – Attempts to reduce officer workloads may serve a dual purpose: They may allow these leaders more time to meaningfully engage with their unit members and be more effective in responding when those in their charge turn to them for advice, information, or other types of assistance for their needs. However, as noted, to truly resolve workload issues, time made available either through reductions in duties, more-efficient processes, additional personnel to accommodate duties, or other strategies should ideally be left as open time. That is, if workload reductions are accompanied by expectations that personnel will then be able to accommodate additional tasks, workloads may not be appreciably reduced.

  – Workload and manpower data already available to the Air Force may reveal in more detail where in the organization airmen need relief in terms of schedules, tasks, and staffing. Recent interviews with squadron commanders found that even units that appear to have sufficient manning may feel understaffed relative to required tasks (Ausink et al., 2018).

- Address sleep-related challenges through multiple avenues because reasons for insufficient or poor-quality sleep can vary. Circumstances that may contribute to sleep-related issues may include heavy work demands or shift work, personal life stressors, behaviors (e.g., too much caffeine, electronics at bedtime), environmental issues (e.g., noise, temperature), and mental or physical health. A recent joint consensus statement of the American Academy of Sleep Medicine and Sleep Research Society asserts that, "Adults should sleep *7 or more* hours per night on a regular basis to promote optimal health" (Watson et al., 2015, p. 591; emphasis in the original). We echo recommendations from recent RAND research on sleep in the military (Troxel et al., 2015), which are still current and applicable here:

  – Across the community: Promote efforts to improve sleep hygiene, time management, and stress management through multiple strategies, such as screening, coaching, instruction, apps, and information campaigns. When personnel are routinely required to work 50 or more hours a week, these strategies should complement leadership efforts to reduce workplace stress and persistently heavy workloads, not substitute for them.

- Among leaders: Educate line leaders on the value of sleep and how to address cultural and environmental barriers to healthy sleep. Include background on the consequences of poor sleep for performance, safety, decisionmaking, and mental and physical health.
- Among health care professionals: Ensure that providers are educated on how to screen for, prevent, and treat sleep disorders.

- Follow-on efforts should seek to better understand perceptions of poor leadership. The specific issues noted with some frequency under the domain of military practices and culture represent a starting point, but detailed local context would be useful for interventions at the local level (i.e., those that do not suggest Air Force–level policy intervention). Such local information may also help direct any change initiatives and be collected using such methodologies as town halls, focus groups, solicitation of input via drop boxes, outreach by chaplains and first sergeants, and review of Total Force Climate Survey results.

- Given the outreach preferences expressed by community members, it may be worthwhile to more systematically facilitate opportunities to opt in or subscribe to having announcements sent to personal email addresses to inform individuals of new programs, or provide information regarding existing programs. This may be particularly useful for reaching guard and reserve members and spouses who are not civilian employees or airmen themselves.

A. Communities for Which Reports Were Prepared

We prepared 2017 Air Force Community Feedback Tool results reports for the following organizations with responsibility for installations across the Air Force:

- Air Combat Command
- Air Education and Training Command
- Air Force District of Washington
- Air Force Global Strike Command
- Air Force Material Command
- Air Force Reserve Command
- Air Force Special Operations Command
- Air Force Space Command
- Air Mobility Command
- Air National Guard
- Pacific Air Forces
- U.S. Air Forces in Europe and Air Forces Africa.

Installation-level results reports were also prepared. This appendix also lists the 161 major active and reserve installations and guard wings that the Air Force Personnel Center has identified as the servicing locations for the Air Force community on and near them. The servicing locations for Air Force personnel assigned to other places, such as joint force headquarters, ROTC units, recruiting stations, other government agencies, and other DoD or military assignments, are Air Force installations in their geographical areas.

Given the purpose of the 2017 Air Force Community Feedback Tool—to inform local policy, programs, and services—a report has been prepared presenting results for each location. At a few of these locations, such as the Pentagon, Fort George Meade, and Joint Base Anacostia-Bolling, the Air Force is not in charge of providing base services. However, these locations have sizable Air Force populations (i.e., well over 2,000) and Community Support Coordinators working to support their needs. Where population sizes and/or response rates were particularly small, the reports contain only top-line results for which there were a sufficient number of respondents.

In this list, a single asterisk indicates an installation at which the Air Force is not in charge of services; two asterisks indicate a remote or isolated installation (as defined in AFI 65-106, p. 14):

1. 101st Air Refueling Wing
2. 102nd Intelligence Wing
3. 103rd Airlift Wing
4. 104th Fighter Wing
5. 105th Airlift Wing
6. 106th Rescue Wing

7. 109th Airlift Wing
8. 110th Attack Wing
9. 111th Attack Wing
10. 114th Fighter Wing
11. 115th Fighter Wing
12. 117th Air Refueling Wing
13. 118th Wing
14. 119th Wing
15. 120th Airlift Wing
16. 121st Air Refueling Wing
17. 122nd Fighter Wing
18. 123rd Airlift Wing
19. 124th Fighter Wing
20. 125th Fighter Wing
21. 127th Wing
22. 128th Air Refueling Wing
23. 129th Rescue Wing
24. 130th Airlift Wing
25. 132nd Wing
26. 134th Air Refueling Wing
27. 137th Special Operations Wing
28. 138th Fighter Wing
29. 139th Airlift Wing
30. 142nd Fighter Wing
31. 143rd Airlift Wing
32. 144th Fighter Wing
33. 145th Airlift Wing
34. 146th Airlift Wing
35. 147th Attack Wing
36. 148th Fighter Wing
37. 151st Air Refueling Wing
38. 152nd Airlift Wing
39. 153rd Airlift Wing
40. 155th Air Refueling Wing
41. 156th Airlift Wing
42. 157th Air Refueling Wing
43. 158th Fighter Wing
44. 159th Fighter Wing
45. 161st Air Refueling Wing
46. 162nd Wing
47. 164th Airlift Wing
48. 165th Airlift Wing
49. 166th Airlift Wing
50. 167th Airlift Wing
51. 169th Fighter Wing
52. 172nd Airlift Wing

53. 173rd Fighter Wing
54. 174th Attack Wing
55. 175th Wing
56. 177th Fighter Wing
57. 178th Wing
58. 179th Airlift Wing
59. 180th Fighter Wing
60. 181st Intelligence Wing
61. 182nd Airlift Wing
62. 183nd Wing
63. 185th Air Refueling Wing
64. 186th Air Refueling Wing
65. 187th Fighter Wing
66. 188th Wing
67. 190th Air Refueling Wing
68. 193rd Special Operations Wing
69. 194th Wing
70. Altus Air Force Base**
71. Aviano Air Base, Italy**
72. Barksdale Air Force Base
73. Beale Air Force Base
74. Buckley Air Force Base, including the 140th Wing
75. Cannon Air Force Base**
76. Columbus Air Force Base
77. Davis-Monthan Air Force Base
78. Dobbins Air Reserve Base
79. Dover Air Force Base
80. Duke Field
81. Dyess Air Force Base
82. Edwards Air Force Base**
83. Eglin Air Force Base
84. Eielson Air Force Base, including the 168th Wing**
85. Ellsworth Air Force Base
86. Fairchild Air Force Base, including the 141st Air Refueling Wing
87. Fort George G. Meade*
88. Francis E. Warren Air Force Base
89. Goodfellow Air Force Base
90. Grand Forks Air Force Base**
91. Grissom Air Reserve Base
92. Hanscom Air Force Base
93. Hill Air Force Base
94. Holloman Air Force Base**
95. Homestead Air Reserve Base
96. Hurlburt Field
97. Incirlik Air Base, Turkey**
98. Joint Base Anacostia-Bolling*

99. Joint Base Andrews, including the 113th Wing
100. Joint Base Charleston
101. Joint Base Elmendorf-Richardson, including the 176th Wing
102. Joint Base Langley-Eustis, including the 192nd Fighter Wing
103. Joint Base Lewis-McChord*
104. Joint Base McGuire-Dix-Lakehurst, including the 108th Wing
105. Joint Base Pearl Harbor-Hickam, including the 154th Wing*
106. Joint Base San Antonio: Fort Sam Houston
107. Joint Base San Antonio: Kelly Field Annex, including the 149th Fighter Wing
108. Joint Base San Antonio: Lackland Air Force Base
109. Joint Base San Antonio: Randolph Air Force Base
110. Joint Region Marianas: Andersen Air Force Base, Guam, including the 254th Air Base Group**
111. Kadena Air Base, Japan**
112. Keesler Air Force Base
113. Kirtland Air Force Base, including the 150th Special Operations Wing
114. Kunsan Air Base, South Korea**
115. Laughlin Air Force Base**
116. Little Rock Air Force Base, including the 189th Airlift Wing
117. Los Angeles Air Force Base
118. Luke Air Force Base
119. MacDill Air Force Base
120. Malmstrom Air Force Base
121. March Air Reserve Base, including the 163rd Attack Wing
122. Maxwell Air Force Base
123. McConnell Air Force Base, including the 184th Intelligence Wing
124. Minneapolis-Saint Paul Joint Air Reserve Station, including the 133rd Airlift Wing
125. Minot Air Force Base**
126. Misawa Air Force Base, Japan**
127. Moody Air Force Base
128. Mountain Home Air Force Base**
129. Naval Air Station Joint Reserve Base Fort Worth, including the 136th Airlift Wing
130. Nellis Air Force Base
131. Niagara Falls Air Reserve Base, including the 107th Attack Wing
132. Offutt Air Force Base
133. Osan Air Force Base, South Korea**
134. Patrick Air Force Base
135. Pentagon*
136. Peterson Air Force Base
137. Pittsburgh Air Reserve Station, including the 171st Air Refueling Wing
138. Pope Field
139. Ramstein Air Base, Germany
140. Robins Air Force Base, including the 116th Air Control Wing
141. Royal Air Force Lakenheath, United Kingdom
142. Royal Air Force Mildenhall, United Kingdom
143. Russell-Knox Building, Quantico

144. Schriever Air Force Base
145. Scott Air Force Base, including the 126th Air Refueling Wing
146. Seymour Johnson Air Force Base
147. Shaw Air Force Base
148. Sheppard Air Force Base
149. Spangdahlem Air Base, Germany
150. Tinker Air Force Base
151. Travis Air Force Base
152. Tyndall Air Force Base
153. U.S. Army Garrison Stuttgart, Germany
154. U.S. Air Force Academy
155. Vance Air Force Base**
156. Vandenberg Air Force Base
157. Westover Air Reserve Base
158. Whiteman Air Force Base, including the 131st Bomb Wing
159. Wright-Patterson Air Force Base
160. Yokota Air Base, Japan
161. Youngstown-Warren Air Reserve Station.

B. Additional Methodological Details and Recommendations

This appendix provides additional information about the framework of the 2017 Air Force Community Feedback Tool, the individual problems the survey asked participants about, marketing used to promote the survey and other methodological considerations, and how and why the survey results presented in this report were weighted to align with the proportion of different demographic subgroups in the Air Force community. It also provides some suggestions for modifications to make in the next survey administration.

Survey Framework

The 2017 Air Force Community Feedback Tool adopted a holistic survey framework developed to assess the needs of service members and their families (Miller et al., 2011; Sims et al., 2017). Subject-matter experts from across the Air Force helped ensure that the survey included appropriate content for active, guard and reserve airmen; their spouses; and Air Force civilian employees, as did reviews of the research literature and other recent surveys. Proposed content was prioritized with the aim of keeping the average survey response time to less than 30 minutes. As shown in Table B.1, the survey first asked respondents to indicate the problems they faced in the past year. Among respondents who indicated more than one *type* of problem, the survey then asked respondents to prioritize the different problem types that they reported experiencing and to identify their most significant type of problem. Respondents who reported at least one problem were then asked about their perceived needs related to the top type of problem, whether they sought help to meet these needs, and how well any resources they used helped in resolving their top problem type. All survey participants were asked to provide their perceptions of military resources designed to be able to assist airmen, their families, or civilian employees with their needs.

The survey also collected information about demographic characteristics, health and well-being, qualities of military resources, and attitudes toward military service or employment from all survey participants. This information provides general information about survey respondents and could be used to further explore characteristics related to the needs of active, guard and reserve airmen; their spouses; and Air Force civilian employees. More-specific descriptions of the survey items used in these analyses are provided throughout the report. Questions concerning the survey instrument may be directed to the lead authors of this report.

Table B.1. Structure of the 2017 Air Force Community Feedback Tool

Survey Section	Which Participants Entered This Survey Section
Screener/branching and key demographic questions	All
Problems in the past year	All
Single most significant problem type	Those who reported having problems that fell across more than one problem type
Needs associated with top problem type	Those who reported having any problems
Ways of meeting greatest needs	Those who reported having any needs for their top type of problem
Satisfaction with ways of meeting greatest needs	Those who contacted at least one military or nonmilitary resource for assistance with their greatest needs for their top type of problem
Qualities of military resources	All
Health and resilience-related measures	All
Attitudes toward military service/employment	All
Additional demographic and background information	All

List of Problems Provided for Each Problem Type

This section provides the list of individual problems, or issues, corresponding to each type of problem on the survey to provide additional context for understanding the survey results. Respondents were asked to indicate all items that had been problems for them in the past year (the past 12 months) or to indicate that they did not experience any of these problems. Except where noted, items were displayed in a random order. These lists are presented here with notations in brackets indicating problems that were presented only to specific demographic subgroups of respondents. The problem types listed below are not necessarily mutually exclusive; the problem types used in the survey are merely one way to categorize problems.

Military Practices and Culture Problems

1. Adjusting to military language, organization, or culture
2. Getting Air Force personnel to listen to you, take you seriously, or treat you with respect
3. Not being able to stay at or go to the military installation you prefer
4. [if airman but not dual military OR if Air Force employee but not also Air Force spouse] Getting accurate information about when you will have to move, deploy, or travel for work
5. [if dual military] Getting accurate information about when you or your spouse will have move, deploy, or travel for work
6. [if military spouse but not dual military] Getting accurate information about when your spouse will have to move, deploy, or travel for work
7. [if airman or employee] Lack of support for your professional/career development
8. [if airman or employee] Poor relationship with coworkers or superiors
9. [if airman or employee] Poor leadership by military personnel in your chain of command
10. [if airman or employee] Poor leadership by civilian personnel in your chain of command
11. [if airman or employee] Your spouse or partner's adjustment to military culture

12. [if dual military] Leadership not understanding the needs of dual military couples
13. [if guard or reserve] Being able to balance civilian employment with your guard and reserve duties
14. [if military spouse but not dual military] Lack of contact with other military spouses
15. [if military spouse but not dual military] Other military spouses not treating you with respect
16. [if employee] Difficulty finding a good Air Force or Department of Defense job
17. [if employee] Military leadership not understanding the civilian workforce
18. [if employee] Military coworkers not valuing civilian workforce contributions
19. [if employee] Inequity regarding bonuses/raises/promotions
20. [if employee AND military spouse] Civilian leadership not understanding military spouses
21. [if employee] Having to use annual leave to participate in unit social activities
22. [if employee] Problems with requests for reasonable workplace accommodations for your disability

Work-Life Balance Problems

1. Finding time for enough sleep, a healthy diet, or physical exercise
2. Finding time to pursue your education
3. Finding time for recreation, stress relief, or family time
4. [if airman] Work hours, schedule, or commute to your military job
5. [if employee or if spouse but NOT dual military] Work hours, schedule, or commute to work
6. [if guard or reserve] Work hours, schedule, or commute to your civilian job
7. Many competing commitments (such as work, school, childcare, volunteer activities)
8. Finding time for social activities outside of work
9. [if Air Force employee] Lack of opportunities for telework or alternative work schedule
10. [if Air Force employee] Getting permission or having to take leave to take care of important errands during the work day

Household Management Problems

1. Moving or storage of belongings
2. Theft, break-in, or vandalism of home or property
3. Transportation or car repair issues
4. Housework or yard work problems
5. Home repairs or work orders for housing

Financial or Legal Problems

1. Pay issues (such as access to pay or errors)
2. [if Air Force guard or reserve] Finding a civilian job that pays enough or offers enough hours
3. [if Air Force employee or if Air Force spouse but not dual military] Finding a job that pays enough or offers enough hours
4. Finding affordable, suitable housing
5. Being able to afford further education

6. Trouble budgeting, paying debt or bills
7. Bankruptcy, foreclosure, repossession of car or other item
8. Power of attorney problems
9. Child custody, divorce, or other family legal problems

Health Care System Problems

[List for airman and Air Force spouses]

1. Poor military health care for new injuries or illnesses
2. Poor military health care for ongoing/long-term injuries or illnesses
3. Poor military health care to manage pregnancy, childbirth, or women's health care
4. Poor military assistance for health behaviors (to help stop smoking, manage weight, manage stress, etc.)
5. Poor military health care to help prevent illness (such as flu or tetanus shots)
6. Poor military health care to screen for problems such as diabetes, high cholesterol, or high blood pressure
7. [if Air Force guard or reserve] Problems transitioning between TRICARE and civilian health systems
8. Getting a timely appointment at a military treatment facility
9. Getting permission to go to a medical appointment during work hours
10. Distance to a military treatment facility
11. Understanding military health benefits
12. Military health insurance claims
13. Cost of nonmilitary health care services [always displayed options 13 and 14 last]
14. Poor nonmilitary health care services

[List for Air Force employee who is not also a spouse]

1. Poor health care for new injuries or illnesses
2. Poor health care for ongoing/long-term injuries or illnesses
3. Poor health care to manage pregnancy, childbirth, or women's health care
4. Poor assistance for health behaviors (to help stop smoking, manage weight, manage stress, etc.)
5. Poor health care to help prevent illness (such as flu or tetanus shots)
6. Poor health care to screen for problems, such as diabetes, high cholesterol, or high blood pressure
7. Getting a timely appointment at a medical treatment facility
8. Getting permission to go to a medical appointment during work hours
9. Understanding your health insurance benefits
10. Health insurance claims

Romantic Relationship Problems

1. [if unmarried] Trouble starting a relationship [always displayed this response option first]
2. Divorce/marital separation/end of relationship
3. Communicating or expressing feelings to one another
4. Growing apart, in different directions
5. Arguments

6. Verbal, physical and/or sexual abuse
7. Infidelity (cheating)
8. Little or no physical affection
9. Changing roles or responsibilities in the family/marriage
10. [if airman or Air Force spouse] Trouble reuniting/reconnecting after a deployment
11. [if airman or Air Force spouse] Problems due to having to be separated during deployment
12. [if married or partnered] Problems due to having to live far away from [if married, insert: "your spouse"] [if partnered, insert: "your partner"]

Child-Specific Problems

[Displayed if respondent has minor children OR did not respond to previous questions about whether they had minor children]

1. [if respondent did not previous indicate whether they had children] Not applicable: I do not have any financially dependent children who are minors [always displayed this response option first]
2. Cost of quality childcare
3. Distance from quality childcare
4. Availability of quality childcare (waiting list, hours, priorities, etc.)
5. Cost of quality youth and teen programs (such as sports, clubs and camps)
6. Distance from quality youth and teen programs
7. Availability of quality youth and teen programs (waiting list, hours, priorities, etc.)
8. Lack of quality, affordable schools for your child
9. Child's poor or dropping grades
10. Conflicting or lack of advice about how best to care for your child
11. Child's emotional or behavior problems
12. [if airman or Air Force spouse] Child's lack of contact with other military children
13. Child's health problems
14. Child's special needs
15. Child's safety problems (bullying, abuse, etc.)
16. Child adjusting after moving or relocation
17. Child adjusting to separation from parent deployed or working far from home

Problems with Your Own Well-Being

1. Feeling stressed or overwhelmed
2. Frequently tired
3. Sleeping problems (too little or too much, nightmares, etc.)
4. Pain, physical injury, or illness
5. Managing your weight
6. Hard to focus, concentrate, or remember things
7. Doing poorly in school or work
8. Work not challenging or doesn't use your skills/education
9. Grieving the loss of a friend or loved one
10. Loneliness or boredom
11. Difficulty finding meaning or purpose in life

12. Mood: depression, impatience, anger, aggression, anxiety
13. Substance misuse or abuse (alcohol, tobacco, drugs)
14. Too much time playing video games, watching TV or movies, or using the Internet or social media (Facebook, Twitter, Snapchat, etc.)
15. Difficulty controlling your spending
16. Challenges due to your physical or learning disability
17. Adapting to living in a foreign country

Problems Your Spouse or Romantic Partner Experienced

[Displayed if respondent is married or partnered]

1. Adjusting to military language, organization, culture
2. Physical health
3. Mental or emotional health
4. Work or school-related problems
5. Conflicts or lack of relationships with other people
6. Difficulty finding meaning or purpose in life
7. Substance misuse or abuse (alcohol, tobacco, drugs)
8. Too much time playing video games, watching TV or movies, or using the Internet or social media (Facebook, YouTube, Instagram, Twitter, Snapchat, etc.)
9. Difficulty controlling their spending
10. Adapting to living in a foreign country

Other Problems

[All respondents were also provided the opportunity to write in a response through the survey item reproduced below.]

If you didn't see a description of a major problem you, your child, or your spouse/partner (if applicable) faced this past year, please briefly describe it here. You'll have a chance at the end of the survey to provide more detail about these or other issues, if you wish.

Please note that we cannot provide confidentiality to a participant regarding comments involving criminal activity/behavior, or statements that pose a threat to yourself or others. Do NOT discuss or comment on classified or operationally sensitive information.

1.
2.
3.

Survey Invitation and Marketing Plan

RAND and Air Force personnel across several organizations partnered to use multiple military and nonmilitary channels to promote awareness of the 2017 Air Force Community Feedback Tool and invite all eligible members of the community (a census) to participate. Targeted messaging with invitations was key. However, as the survey was going out to a community census, general marketing was also a relevant mode of communication with potential respondents. Across the targeted and general messaging, the communication about the survey used varying modes, lengths, formal and informal tones, and text and images to diversify and broaden their appeal and reach. Common themes emphasized that community members could influence change, that the Air Force was seeking input on whether it was meeting the needs of its community, that feedback from diverse types of community members was needed, and that the survey presents an opportunity to help shape what is available to the Air Force community.

Survey Incentives

OPA surveys both service members and spouses but does not provide monetary incentives to service members and spouses because of the costs for large surveys and legal constraints, which are described in further detail below by population. However, given that incentives have been found to increase response rates in other surveys, OPA suggests the possibility of requesting legislative relief from the legal constraints, and to contain costs, perhaps using incentives to target hard-to-reach populations (such as junior enlisted) (OPA, 2018e).

Personnel

Survey incentives were not offered to Air Force personnel for several reasons. The most important reason is that, by law, federal personnel (which includes both service members and civilian employees) cannot receive compensation for participating in an Air Force, DoD, or federal survey while they are on duty, as that would constitute double compensation for their time (OPA, 2018e; DoD Instruction 3216.02, 2011). It would introduce a hurdle to participation to send the survey invitation to work email addresses and offer incentives for participation, yet instruct everyone to forward their emails to their personal addresses to take the survey later, when not on duty.[42] Additionally, some military leaders have considered providing feedback to military leadership as falling within the realm of service members' responsibilities rather than as additional work requiring additional compensation, and have therefore objected to incentives on principle. Unconditional gifts could be proposed, but when surveying enough personnel to support reporting at the installation level, the cost would be prohibitive; there were 637,831 eligible personnel in July 2017. Providing incentives to only segments of the population introduces issues of fairness. Finally, for incentives to be lawful, the Air Force would have to demonstrate that this use of appropriated funds meets the "necessary expense rule" (GAO, 2017). Not having previously administered this survey and exhausted other possible strategies to increase the survey response rate, there would have been and likely still is insufficient

---

[42] This strategy would also introduce an ethical issue in the sense of providing personnel (who, to receive compensation, could not then take the survey during duty hours) the temptation to take the survey while on duty and raise the potential risk of harm if they were to be observed doing so.

information to make the legal case that incentives are necessary for this particular survey at this time.

Spouses

We were able to obtain legal approval for providing small incentives to spouses for survey completion. The postcard for spouses noted that a modest $2 Amazon.com gift code was being offered to civilian spouses of airmen as an optional token of appreciation for completion of the survey. At the end of the survey, spouses were provided instructions on how they could claim this gift code by providing an email address for gift code receipt that would be stored securely on the survey vendor server in a file separate from all survey responses, so it could not be linked. The offer also explained that the list of email addresses would be used only to award gift codes and would be saved only as long as necessary for the special promotion. Approximately one-third of participating spouses chose to request a gift code.

Targeted Messaging

Personalized messages sent to individual community members included the following:

- Digitally signed, personalized survey invitations AFSO sent to the official email addresses of Air Force personnel, using an "af.mil" email address marked as being sent on behalf of the Assistant Vice Chief of Staff. Emails were sent at the beginning of August 2017, with reminder messages sent at the beginning and end of September.
- Postcards addressed "To the spouse of" married airmen whose spouses are not airmen themselves, mailed at the beginning of August 2017 to the airman's home address of record. Postcards were sent via first class mail so that they could be forwarded if a forwarding address were on record with the post office. We considered direct emails to spouses, but AFSO does not have direct contact information for them, and the process for obtaining such information from DoD would have extended beyond the Air Force's desired time frame for a survey launch. So, emails to spouses were not part of the recruiting strategy for this administration.

Broader Marketing

RAND and Air Force representatives from across the organization contributed to numerous and varied strategies to market the survey through a range of channels. Marketing materials and efforts included the following:

- A command support letter was prepared and signed by the Assistant Vice Chief of Staff that could be distributed or posted along with other messages.
- RAND hosted an informational survey webpage that contained the command support letter; a link to the survey; and frequently asked questions, which included examples of actions that resulted from past community survey feedback to illustrate the usefulness of prior surveys in concrete, accessible terms (RAND Corporation, 2017).
- RAND graphic artists prepared marketing images in formats and ratios to fit 8.5 × 11 flyers, Facebook, Twitter, and websites. These images included a range of Air Force

photographs depicting officers and enlisted airmen, civilian employees, men and women, racial diversity, families and individuals, and various apparent occupations (e.g., pilot, security forces, aircraft maintenance, not determinable). To support local marketing efforts, these were available on the survey information website and on an internal Air Force community-of-practice website. Internet searches during the survey administration period revealed that several bases were using these images on open websites or social media platforms.

- The Air Force project action officer prepared an Air Force marketing toolkit that was posted on an internal Air Force community of practice website and distributed to base points of contact. The toolkit included informational slides, examples of social media post or email language describing the survey, a page on key talking points, the command support letter, and the marketing images.

- The Air Force project action officer briefed a gathering of base Community Support Coordinators (who can help promote the survey locally) prior to the survey launch.

- The Airman and Family Care Division provided information to all the Airman and Family Readiness Centers across the Air Force about the survey and asking them to promote it in their communities.

- An announcement was made via Air Force TV (viewable on YouTube, at the end of this broadcast: U.S. Air Force, 2017).

- The Secretary of the Air Force Public Affairs office posted a news release on the Air Force Portal website that contained a link to the survey.

- A banner, or icon, for the survey rotated on the top of the Air Force Portal website for several weeks during the survey. Clicking on the banner would take the users to the Air Force Public Affairs news release page.

- RAND's Office of External Affairs sent a press release to news outlets that might have a substantial Air Force audience (e.g., *Air Force Times*, *Stars and Stripes*, and outlets in communities with Air Force installations).

- Local installations sent emails, flyers, social media posts, and meeting announcements advertising the survey or providing reminders and encouraging participation.

- An Air Force–staffed helpdesk enabled community members to contact someone at an official Air Force email address (ending in "af.mil") or a military phone number (defense switched network, more commonly known as "DSN") to verify the legitimacy of the survey effort. In addition, a RAND-staffed helpdesk could be used to report access or other technical issues with the survey.

Survey Mode

The survey was web-based, which is practical and affordable for surveying a population of this size and is standard for large-scale military surveys. Paper and phone call survey options were not offered as additional survey modes for several reasons, although the Air Force may wish to reconsider this choice in future administrations.

Because of the complex branching the survey used to follow needs resulting from problems, resources contacted to try to meet needs, and helpfulness of the resources contacted, a paper survey would have had to either omit core survey questions or be very lengthy and confusing for recipients to follow, thus introducing the possibility of many survey errors and less useable data. A paper survey would also have required a great deal of additional expense to format, print, mail, provide return mailing and postage, and process received surveys. More generally, it was unclear whether adding a paper survey would have provided a meaningful return on investment (National Research Council, 2013). We also considered DoD's experience, which suggests that it would be hard to justify the expense:

> Beginning with the first test of the SOFS [Status of Forces Survey] in 2002, DMDC has periodically included tests of methodology differences affecting response rates and data quality. Such tests have concluded that a follow-up paper survey increases response rates by around seven percentage points without significantly or meaningfully changing estimates from the survey. (letter from Mary Snavely-Dixon, reproduced in U.S. Government Accountability Office, 2010, p. 6)

Another potentially more feasible mode would be phone participation. In the research that developed the basic framework that provided the foundation for the development of the 2017 Air Force Community Feedback Tool, service members and spouses were offered two survey participation modes (Miller et al., 2011). They could participate in the web survey or could call a number at a time convenient to them to participate by phone. The option to phone in rather than have survey administrators call potential respondents eliminated a number of methodological issues, such as the challenges of obtaining current and accurate phone numbers, the risk of annoying or angering individuals who do not want to be called for survey solicitation, the potential for waking individuals or having them respond while driving, and the potential for recipients to incur charges (e.g., if they use a prepaid mobile phone). All survey promotion materials informed service members and spouses that they could take the survey over the phone by calling the toll-free number any day of the week between 6 a.m. and 9 p.m. All 699 respondents, however, chose the web-based survey mode (Miller et al., 2011, p. 52). Given that experience, we did not propose a phone option for the 2017 survey. However, given the technological hurdles that some Air Force personnel encountered accessing the "dot com" survey website from their Air Force network computer and that not all personnel have easy access to computers in their work environment, the feasibility of a phone option for future survey administration should be explored.

A Note About Response Rates

Low response rates can sometimes be a concern if those who do participate in a survey differ in important ways from those who do not (*nonresponse bias*). However, as noted in Chapter 1, there is no set scientific standard for a minimal response rate for a survey to be valid or to designate it as representative or free from nonresponse bias. DoD survey response rates have been trending downward, as have survey participation rates more generally (OPA, 2018e; Miller and Aharoni, 2015; National Research Council, 2013). Strategies to increase response rates, such as using multiple modes, have not always demonstrated a compelling return on investment as described above. At the same time, empirical assessments of surveys research have been finding that, "the response rate of a survey may not be as strongly associated with the quality or representativeness of the survey as had been generally believed" (Johnson and Wislar, 2012, p. 1805; see also Groves, 2006; Groves and Peytcheva, 2008).

As further context for understanding these response rates, we look to airmen's and Air Force spouses' participation in DoD's 2017 spouse surveys and service member Status of Forces surveys. DoD invited a sample of airmen and spouses to participate (not the entire eligible population). DoD mailed a survey notification letter to the sample and emailed a survey invitation (OPA, 2018a; OPA, 2018b; OPA, 2018c; OPA, 2018d). Spouses and reserve airmen were also sent postal reminders, and spouses who did not initially respond via the web were mailed paper surveys (OPA, 2018a; OPA, 2018b; OPA, 2018c; OPA, 2018d).

Ultimately, greater *numbers* of airmen and Air Force spouses responded to the Air Force Community Feedback Tool, but greater *percentages* of the samples responded to the DoD surveys:[43]

- The total number of Air Force spouses who participated in the 2017 DoD active and reserve component spouse surveys was 4,664, and their response rates were 17% of active component, 19% of guard, and 15% of reserve Air Force spouses in the sample (OPA 2018d, p. 8; 2018e, p. 7). In contrast, 7,434 Air Force spouses participated in the 2017 Air Force Community Feedback Tool, which was 3% of the overall Air Force spouse population. Thus, 2,770 more Air Force spouses participated in the Air Force survey than in the DoD survey(s).
- The total number of airmen who participated in the 2017 DoD Status of Forces active and reserve component surveys was 8,475, and response rates were 21% of active, 18% of guard, and 15% of reserve airmen in the sample (OPA 2018b p. 14; 2018 p. 12). In contrast, 56,633 airmen participated in the 2017 Air Force Community Feedback tool, which was 13% of active, 10% of guard, and 7% of reserve airmen in the overall population. Thus, more than six times as many airmen participated in the Air Force survey than in these DoD survey(s).

Adjusting for Survey Nonresponse Among Air Force Personnel

Survey nonresponse results in a loss of sample size that reduces the precision of estimates. Nonresponse can also cause bias if the attitudes, experiences, and indicators from respondents are systematically different from the (unobserved) attitudes, experiences, and indicators of nonrespondents. For example, this would occur if survey respondents tended to have fewer (or

---

[43] For further discussion of response rates across various surveys of DoD service members and spouses, see Miller and Aharoni, 2015, and OPA, 2018e. It does not appear that OPA conducted a DoD civilian employee survey in this time frame.

different) needs than survey nonrespondents did. We adjusted survey outcomes to reduce potential bias.

Responses from Air Force personnel—airmen and civilian employees—were weighted to be representative of certain observable characteristics of personnel at their base. These weights account for differences in the characteristics of survey respondents compared with the overall community of Air Force personnel at each location. This adjustment is important when respondents are not representative of the overall community (because some demographic subgroups are more likely to participate than others) and when characteristics of respondents are related to the survey results. For example, if survey respondents tended to have a higher pay grade than the overall community and if personnel at higher pay grades had different needs from personnel at lower pay grades, unweighted statistics would be skewed toward the needs of high-pay-grade personnel and so would not reflect the overall needs of Air Force personnel.

Estimating Nonresponse Weights for Air Force Personnel

We used logistic regression models to estimate the relationship between the characteristics of surveyed individuals and the probability of responding to the survey and to estimate nonresponse weights. Air Force personnel identified as *survey respondents* fulfilled completion requirements: They provided key demographic characteristics required to proceed through the survey and either indicated problems they had experienced in the past year or confirmed that they had experienced no problems.

Characteristics Included in Response Models

Models describe survey response at the person level and include both respondents and nonrespondents, so characteristics used to identify and adjust for differences between respondents and nonrespondents must be available for *all* Air Force personnel. These characteristics were drawn from the Air Force Personnel Data Center personnel file. The characteristics we used for weighting Air Force personnel were Air Force status (active component, guard, reserve) or civilian employee status (nonappropriated or appropriated fund civilian employee), gender, pay grade group (military or the civilian equivalent), education level, and race or ethnicity. Characteristics of airmen also included any military dependents under the age 18 and marital status (married to an airman, married to someone else, unmarried). Characteristics of civilian employees also included veteran status and guard or reserve status. Employees who had previously been active component airmen but were guard or reserve airmen at the time of the survey were not categorized as military veterans because they were still airmen. Table B.2 describes nonresponse predictors. For airmen models, we also included an interaction between gender and pay grade. Because we have different types of information for the airmen and civilian employee populations, we fit two separate response models for these groups.

Table B.2. Characteristics Included in Survey Response Models for Air Force Personnel

Characteristic	Airmen Model	Civilian Employee Model
Air Force status:	Yes	Yes
Not an airman, active component, guard, or reserve		
Air Force civilian employee status:		
Not a civilian employee, civilian employee	Yes	No
Nonappropriated fund civilian employee, appropriated fund civilian employee: General Schedule, appropriated fund civilian employee: Federal Wage System, other type of appropriated fund civilian employee	No	Yes
Gender (woman)	Yes	Yes
Education level:	Yes	Yes
High school diploma or equivalent, some college, associate's degree or certificate, bachelor's degree, graduate or professional degree, other/unknown)		
Marital status:	Yes	No
Married to an airman, married to someone who is not an airman, unmarried)		
Military pay grade group (a categorical variable with three groups):	Yes	No
Junior enlisted (E1–E4), NCO (E5–E9), and officer (O1–O10)		
Gender by military pay grade group (interaction between these variables)	Yes	No
Military career group (ten categories):	Yes	No
Acquisition, logistics/maintenance, medical, operations, professional, special duty, special investigations, support, other, missing)		
Military dependents under the age of 18:	Yes	No
Yes or no		
Race:	Yes	No
White, black, Asian, American Indian or Native Hawaiian, multiracial, declined to provide		
Ethnicity:	Yes	No
Hispanic, not Hispanic, declined to provide		
Veteran Status:	No	Yes
Yes or no		

Logistic Regression Models for Survey Response

Because the survey data are clustered within installations, we estimated the relationship between response and Air Force personnel characteristics using a fixed effects model that included an installation effect:

$$logit\left(P\left(r_{ij} = 1|x_{ij}\right)\right) = \beta_{0i} + x_{ij}\beta_1,$$

where r_{ij} indicates the response for the jth person within the ith installation and is 1 for survey respondents and 0 for nonrespondents; x_{ij} represents person-level characteristics; and β_{0i} is an installation-level effect used to account for potential differences in response probabilities across installations (Skinner and D'Arrigo, 2011).

133

Findings from Response Weight Models

Overall response rates were 11.7% among airmen ($N = 56{,}368$ respondents) and 16.2% among civilian employees ($N = 27{,}071$ respondents). There was considerable overlap in the distribution of the predicted probability of response for individuals who did and did not respond to the survey. The area under the receiver operating characteristic curve (area under the curve, AUC) provides a simple comparison of the distributions of estimated probabilities for respondent and nonrespondents. The AUC ranges from 0.5 to 1.0, with 0.5 indicating perfect overlap between the distributions, and 1.0 indicating complete separation of the distributions. The AUC was 0.67 for airmen and 0.66 for civilian employees. Among Air Force personnel who are both guard or reserve airmen and civilian employees, the overall response rate was 12.1% ($N = 1{,}602$ respondents among $N = 13{,}200$). Among the airmen who were also civilian employees, the airmen and civilian employee models were similarly accurate, with an AUC of 0.58 for the airmen model and 0.60 for the civilian employee model. Thus, we used response weights estimated from the civilian model for dual-status airmen because their responses were included with the installation report corresponding to their civilian place of employment.

All the characteristics included in response models were statistically significant predictors of response. Details regarding characteristics related to survey response are discussed in the following paragraphs.

Nonresponse Weights

Nonresponse weights were estimated based on the inverse probability that an individual with a given set of characteristics would respond to the survey. These nonresponse weights give more weight to people who were unlikely to respond than people who were likely to respond. Estimating these response probabilities is key to estimating nonresponse weights. Theoretically, people who respond and have a low probability of response represent more nonresponders in the population than people who respond and have a high probability of response.

We estimated response probabilities using two models (one for airmen and another for civilian employees). The civilian employee model excluded 12 installations with fewer than ten civilian employees (all stand-alone guard wings); installation-level response probabilities could not be estimated because of small sample sizes.

For each person, we estimated nonresponse probabilities based on the inverse logit function, given by

$$p_{ij} = logit^{-1}(\hat{\beta}_{0i} + x_{ij}\hat{\beta}_1),$$

where $\hat{\beta}_{0i}$ is an installation-specific intercept term. We were unable to estimate response probabilities for a few airmen ($N = 1{,}069$) and civilian employees ($N = 16$) because of incomplete data (this includes 11 Air Force personnel with incomplete data who were both

134

airmen and civilian employees). We estimated response probabilities for these personnel using the response fraction[44] at their assigned installation.

Raw nonresponse weights are equal to the inverse response probability of response:

$$w_{ij} = \frac{1}{p_{ij}}.$$

For each installation, final nonresponse weights were rescaled so that the sum of the weights assigned to airmen at the location is equal to the number of airmen at that location and so that the sum of the weights assigned to civilian employees is equal to the number of civilian employees. Weights were rescaled separately for three groups: airmen who were not civilian employees, airmen who were also civilian employees, and civilian employees who were not airmen. Because weights sum to population sizes (based on personnel files), they were scaled to provide summaries that are representative of these three groups at each installation, MAJCOM, or DRU and at the overall Air Force level.

Estimated Nonresponse Weights

The average nonresponse weight for Air Force personnel was 7.8. The SD of nonresponse weights was 5.6; weights ranged from 2.2 to 154 for airmen and from 1.3 to 48.9 for civilian employees. While the range of nonresponse weights is wide for airmen, relatively few airmen had very large weights (as reflected by the SD). When weights span a wide range, weighted estimates can be imprecise, and analysts may improve precision (while potentially increasing bias) by truncating weights (Cole and Hernán, 2008). Because the focus of our reports was on descriptive results, we did not modify the weights used in these analyses.

Models Describing Nonresponse as a Function of Individual and Installation Characteristics

We conducted additional analysis of survey response as a function of individual and installation-level characteristics, based on a logistic regression model:

$$logit\left(P\left(r_{ij} = 1 \middle| x_{ij}, z_j\right)\right) = \beta_0 + x_{ij}\beta_1 + z_j\beta_2,$$

where r_{ij} indicates response of the jth person within the ith installation; x_{ij} gives person-level characteristics shown in Table B.2; and z_j gives installation-level characteristics. Installation characteristics include whether the base is at a U.S. location, whether it is a joint base, whether it is Air Force led, whether it is a stand-alone guard wing installation (i.e., not part of an active or reserve base), whether the base is in a remote and isolated location (as defined by AFI 65-106, 2009), and whether the base was located in an area affected by a hurricane during the survey administration period of August–October 2017 (i.e., in Texas, Florida, Alabama, Georgia, North Carolina, South Carolina, Puerto Rico, or the U.S. Virgin Islands).

We estimated two different models for Air Force personnel response probabilities: one for airmen and another for civilian employees. We used generalized estimating equations to estimate

---

[44] The *response fraction* is the percentage who responded divided by 100 and so ranges from 0 to 1.

population-average effects of individual- and installation-level characteristics on response probabilities and to account for clustering of respondents within installations. Standard errors were estimated using an independence working correlation matrix with a robust covariance adjustment. For example, using this approach, results from the airmen model provide an estimated odds ratio that compares the probability of response for active airmen relative to guard or reserve airmen.

Findings from Nonresponse Models

Nonresponse models focused on the characteristics related to response rather than on estimation of weights. These models excluded 1,069 (0.2%) airmen and 16 (< 0.1%) civilian employees with missing demographic information. Model results in terms of odds ratios and 95% confidence intervals (CIs) are shown in Table B.3. The comparison group (reference group) is the largest group.

Table B.3. Results from Nonresponse Models that Describe the Association Between Individual- and Installation-Level Characteristics and Air Force Personnel Survey Participation

	Airmen Model		Civilian Employee Model	
	Odds Ratio	95% CI	Odds Ratio	95% CI
Location characteristics				
Foreign country location (vs. U.S. location)	1.02	(0.93, 1.13)	1.06	(0.93, 1.21)
Joint base (vs. not)	0.98	(0.87, 1.25)	1.09	(0.98, 1.22)
Not Air Force led (vs. Air Force led)	1.01	(0.82, 1.25)	1.19	(0.97, 1.47)
Stand-alone guard wing (vs. not)	1.02	(0.90, 1.16)	1.26	(0.90, 1.76)
Remote and isolated location (vs. not)	1.07	(0.96, 1.19)	1.30	(1.19, 1.41)
In a hurricane impacted area (vs. not)	0.87	(0.80, 0.94)	0.96	(0.87, 1.07)
Individual characteristics				
Airman status (relative to active component)				
Air National Guard	0.44	(0.41, 0.48)		
Air Force Reserve	0.65	(0.58, 0.74)		
Employee status (relative to appropriated fund: General Schedule)				
Appropriated fund: Federal Wage System			0.59	(0.50, 0.69)
Other appropriated			0.85	(0.79, 0.91)
Nonappropriated fund			0.28	(0.24, 0.33)
Military veteran (vs. not)			1.57	(1.47, 1.67)

136

	Airmen Model		Civilian Employee Model	
	Odds Ratio	**95% CI**	**Odds Ratio**	**95% CI**
Dual status of airman and civilian employee (vs. not)	1.54	(1.45, 1.65)	0.96	(0.87, 1.07)
Gender (women vs. men)	1.21	(1.17, 1.26)	1.22	(1.15, 1.28)
Education level (airmen relative to some college, civilians relative to high school diploma or equivalent)				
High school diploma or equivalent	0.41	(0.34, 0.51)	1.00	
Some college	1.00		1.24	(1.15, 1.34)
Associate's degree or certificate	1.45	(1.41, 1.49)	1.52	(1.44, 1.60)
Bachelor's degree	1.66	(1.60, 1.73)	1.55	(1.47, 1.63)
Graduate or professional degree	2.32	(2.18, 2.46)	1.91	(1.81, 2.03)
Other/Unknown	0.71	(0.60, 0.84)	0.76	(0.67, 0.85)
Race (relative to White)				
Black	0.73	(0.71, 0.76)		
Asian	0.97	(0.91, 1.03)		
American Indian or Native Hawaiian	0.88	(0.82, 0.95)		
Multiracial	1.00	(0.95, 1.04)		
Declined to Provide	0.87	(0.83, 0.92)		
Ethnicity (relative to not Hispanic)				
Hispanic	0.85	(0.82, 0.87)		
Declined to provide	0.87	(0.83, 0.92)		
Marital status (relative to married to someone who is not an airman)				
Not married	0.78	(0.75, 0.80)		
Married to an airman	0.90	(0.87, 0.93)		
Military dependents under the age 18 (vs. none)	0.98	(0.95, 1.00)		
Military pay grade group (relative to NCO: E5–E9)				
Junior enlisted (E1–E4)	0.49	(0.47, 0.52)		
Officer (O1–O10)	0.68	(0.64, 0.71)		
Gender by military pay grade group[a] (relative to NCO women)				
Junior enlisted women	1.59	(1.49, 1.69)		
Officer women	1.05	(0.99, 1.11)		
Military career group variable (relative to logistics/maintenance)				

	Airmen Model		Civilian Employee Model	
	Odds Ratio	95% CI	Odds Ratio	95% CI
Acquisition	1.05	(0.95, 1.16)		
Medical	0.96	(0.91, 1.02)		
Operations	0.88	(0.83, 0.92)		
Professional	1.11	(1.00, 1.23)		
Special duty	1.05	(0.96, 1.16)		
Special investigations	0.69	(0.57, 0.83)		
Support	0.99	(0.95, 1.03)		
Other	0.75	(0.66, 0.87)		

[a] Tested using an interaction between these variables.

Airmen who were located at installations in hurricane-affected areas were significantly less likely than other personnel to participate in the survey. Civilian employees at installations in remote and isolated locations were significantly more likely than other employees to respond. None of the other installation characteristics included in the model were significantly associated with survey response.

Women (among both airmen and civilian employees) were significantly more likely to respond than men. Among airmen who are men, the probability of response was lower for both junior enlisted men and officers than for NCO men. The effect of rank group differed for women; junior enlisted women were more likely to respond than were NCO women. In contrast, both junior enlisted men and male officers were less likely to respond to the survey than NCO men.

Education was also associated with response probability for both airmen and civilians, with higher levels of education corresponding with greater likelihood of participation.

The probability of survey response among airmen was associated with component, race, ethnicity, and marital status. Guard and reserve members were less likely to respond than active component airmen. Airmen who are black, American Indian or Native Hawaiian, or Hispanic or who declined to provide their race or ethnicity for Air Force personnel records were less likely to respond to the survey than other airmen. Airmen who were unmarried or married to an airman were less likely to respond than airmen married to someone other than an airman. There were few significant differences in response rates by military career group. None of these characteristics were available for civilian employees.

Among civilian employees, appropriated fund General Schedule employees were more likely to respond than were other types of employees, and veterans were more likely to respond than were civilian employees who are not veterans.

Adjusting for Survey Nonresponse Among Spouses of Airmen Who Are Not Airmen Themselves

Three groups were invited to participate in the survey: airmen, civilian employees, and spouses of airmen. Spouses—individuals who are married to airmen—could be airmen themselves. Results from spouses, described here, are restricted to nonairman spouses. The Air Force Personnel Center did not have a list of Air Force spouses (names, contact information, characteristics of themselves and their airmen) to provide to us, and we did not have time within the survey time frame with to go through all the steps necessary to obtain such a file from the DoD Manpower Data Center.

From the personnel file, we were able to identify which airmen were married to individuals who were not also airmen ($N = 223{,}498$). We mailed postcards about the survey addressed "to the spouse of" these airmen to the home mailing addresses of the married airmen. Each postcard contained a unique survey access code for that spouse. At the same time, Air Force civilian employees were emailed an invitation to the survey containing a survey link and a unique survey access code. Because we could not identify from the personnel records which civilian employees were also spouses of airmen (the Air Force Personnel Center does not track this), spouses who are civilian employees may have been invited twice with two different survey access codes that cannot be linked.

Based on survey responses, 835 respondents who accessed the survey using a civilian employee access code reported that they were married to airmen (2.9% of the 28,683 respondents who used a civilian employee survey access code). Among respondents who accessed the survey using a spouse access code, 71 reported that they were also Air Force civilian employees (1.1% of the 6,743 respondents who used a spouse survey access code). Thus, in total, we obtained 7,716 surveys from Air Force spouses who are not airmen themselves. As we describe later, the overall response rate among nonairman spouses was less than 3.5%. In light of this low response rate, we expect that very few civilian employees who are also spouses of airmen responded to the survey twice.

The methods used to adjust nonairman spouses' results for survey response parallel methods used for Air Force personnel survey response. Spouse respondents who were not airmen themselves used either a civilian employee survey access code or a spouse survey access code to enter the survey. Because we focused on nonairman spouses, we excluded all spouses who responded using an airman code. For the 87.7% of nonairman spouses who accessed the survey using a spouse access code, we have all the information needed about their airmen to estimate nonresponse models.[45] We lack information about spouses' airmen for the 12.3% of nonairman spouse respondents who accessed the survey using a civilian employee access code (which allowed us to link them to their civilian employee characteristics but not to match them to their

---

[45] The data, based on personnel files, are available in appendix Table C.1.

airmen). For these spouses, who are also civilians, we have their own civilian employee information but not their airmen's. For all spouse respondents, regardless of which code they used to access the survey, we have survey responses indicating their airmen's military status and the number of dependents they have under the age of 18.

Adjustments for Survey Response

Estimation of response probabilities requires information that is available for all spouses, including

- all nonrespondent spouses
- spouse respondents who accessed the survey using a survey access code mailed to nonairman spouses
- spouse respondents who accessed the survey using a survey access code emailed to them because they are also civilian employees.

Use of Different Data Sources

When estimating nonresponse probabilities, our ideal goal would be to use the same information sources for respondents and nonrespondents from the same point in time. We used data from the personnel file for 99.6% of the spouse population, including nonrespondents and respondents who accessed the survey using a spouse access code. For spouse respondents who accessed the survey using a civilian employee access code, we used the best available information: survey data that aligned with personnel file data.

Two survey items correspond to the information contained in personnel files, so we were able to use these two variables—available for all spouses—to predict nonairman spouse survey response: airman's military status (active, guard or reserve) and dependents under the age of 18. Additionally, the survey access code allowed us to use a location variable: for nonrespondents and respondents who used the spouse access code, this is the location that services their airmen. For the spouses who used the civilian access code, the code is linked to the location that services them as civilian employees (as we do not have visibility on their airman's characteristics).

Before using the survey data on airman status and dependents from the spouses who used their civilian employee survey access code, we compared survey and personnel file results among spouse respondents who used the spouse survey access code. We found good agreement between personnel file data and survey reports for both their airmen's military status (94% agreement) and dependents under 18 (89% agreement). For their airmen's military status, 99% of those identified as the spouse of an active component airman from personnel files reported the same military status on the survey; 83% of those identified as a guard spouse reported the same on the survey; and 87% identified as a reserve spouse reported the same on the survey. The greater discrepancy among guard and reserve spouses could result from airmen transitioning from active to reserve status between the time the personnel data files were drawn (July 2017) and the point at which the spouses participated in the survey (August to early October 2017) and/or from spouses confusing active duty status with active component membership.

Regarding dependents, 75% of respondent spouses identified in the personnel files as not having military dependents under 18 also reported not having dependents on the survey, and 98% of those identified as having military dependents under 18 in the personnel files also reported having dependents on the survey. The greater discrepancy for those recorded as *not* having children could reflect the birth or adoption of children between the time the personnel data files were drawn (July 2017) and the time the spouse participated in the survey (August to early October 2017),

Creating Deduplicated Response Data for Nonairman Spouses

Nonairman spouses could have accessed the survey via one of two pathways: using their spouse survey code or, if they were also civilian employees, using their civilian survey code. Spouses who accessed the survey via the spouse survey code are linked to their airman's information, and are therefore easily identifiable as spouse "responders." Spouses who accessed the survey using their civilian survey code cannot be linked to their airmen's data. Furthermore, they are counted twice in the data set: once as a respondent (from the personnel data) and once as a *nonrespondent* (from their unlinked spouse record). Thus, without considering this issue, we would underestimate the response rate in spouses and, specifically, for nonairman spouses who are civilian employees.

Because we could not link nonairman spouses to their airmen's data, we used frequency matching to remove duplicated individuals from the nonairman spouse population data. For each location, ℓ, we adjusted the number of nonairman spouses who were nonrespondents using up to six possible spouse groups, g, as shown in Table B.4. Not all groups were present at every location, which was particularly the case for stand-alone guard wings (those not located on an active or reserve base).

**Table B.4. Six Spouse Groups Used to Adjust Survey
Response Rates in the Models for Spouses**

Spouse Group	Characteristics
Spouse of active airman	No dependents under the age of 18
	One or more dependents under the age of 18
Spouse of guard airman	No dependents under the age of 18
	One or more dependents under the age of 18
Spouse of reserve airman	No dependents under the age of 18
	One or more dependents under the age of 18

There are three counts for each of these groups:

- $N_{\ell gT}$ = the total number of nonairman spouses from the personnel file
- $N_{\ell gS}$ = the number of spouse respondents who accessed the survey using their spouse survey code, which was mailed to all nonairman spouses
- $N_{\ell gE}$ = the number of spouse respondents who are also civilian employees and who accessed the survey using their civilian employee code, which was emailed to all civilian employees.

The combined file used to estimate response weights (described in the next section) has $N_{\ell gT} + N_{\ell gE}$ records in each group. Therefore, to accurately estimate the response rates, we removed $N_{\ell gE}$ nonresponding nonairman spouses at random from each group. Nonresponse models are based on location, status of their airmen (active, guard, or reserve), and dependents under 18, with $N_{\ell gS} + N_{\ell gE}$ respondents in each group and $N_{\ell gT} - N_{\ell gS} - N_{\ell gE}$ nonrespondents in each group.

Estimation of Response Weights

We used logistic regression models to estimate the probability of survey response as a function of location, airman's military status, and dependents under 18. Models included a fixed installation-level effect to capture potential overall differences in spouse response rates across installations.

For each spouse of an airman who was not also an airman, we estimated nonresponse probabilities based on the inverse logit function. We were unable to estimate response probabilities for a few nonairman spouses ($N = 46$) because of incomplete data. We used the response fraction at their assigned installation to estimate response probabilities for these individuals. Response probabilities were then estimated using the inverse logit function. Raw nonresponse weights were estimated as one over the probability of nonresponse. These raw weights were rescaled to sum to the number of nonairman spouses within each installation. Because weights sum to population sizes (based on personnel files), they are scaled to provide summaries representative of the size of these nonairman spouses at the installation, MAJCOM or DRU, and overall Air Force levels.

Findings from Response Weight Models

The overall response rate was 3.3% among nonairman spouses ($N = 7,434$). There was considerable overlap in the distribution of the predicted response probability for spouses who did and did not respond to the survey. The AUC provides a simple comparison of the distributions of estimated probabilities for respondent and nonrespondents. The AUC ranges from 0.5 to 1.0, with 0.5 indicating perfect overlap between the distributions and 1.0 indicating complete separation. The AUC was 0.58 for nonairman spouses.

142

The airman's military status was statistically significant predictor of the spouse responding to the survey, but having military dependents under 18 was not a significant predictor.

Estimated Nonresponse Weights

The average nonresponse weight for nonairman spouses was 30 (SD = 9). Nonresponse weights ranged from 13.6 to 94.6. The range of weights suggests that the variability of estimates might be reduced by trimming the weights. However, this comes at the cost of potentially increasing bias. Because the focus of installation, MAJCOM, DRU and the Air National Guard reports was on descriptive results, we did not modify (trim) the weights used in our analyses of spouse outcomes.

Models Describing Nonresponse as a Function of Individual and Installation Characteristics

Using the same approach we employed to understand factors associated with nonresponse among Air Force personnel, we examined nonresponse among spouses of airmen who are not airmen themselves. Recall that less information was available about spouses, so we could not examine differences by spouse gender, education, or other characteristics that were available for airmen or employees. As shown in Table B.5, spouses with airmen assigned to installations in foreign countries and at joint bases were less likely than other spouses to respond to the survey. Spouses of airmen in the Air National Guard and Air Force Reserve were less likely to respond than spouses whose airmen were active component airmen.

Table B.5. Results from Nonresponse Models That Describe the Association Between Individual- and Installation-Level Characteristics and Spouse Survey Participation

	Odds Ratio	95% CI
Location Characteristics		
Foreign country location (vs. U.S. location)	0.72	(0.61, 0.85)
Joint base (vs. not)	0.86	(0.76, 0.97)
Not Air Force led (vs. Air Force led)	1.15	(0.93, 1.42)
Stand-alone guard wing (vs. not)	1.16	(0.95, 1.41)
Remote and isolated location (vs. not)	0.92	(0.79, 1.07)
In a hurricane impacted area (vs. not)	0.99	(0.89, 1.10)
Individual Characteristics		
Status of their airmen (relative to active component)		
Air National Guard	0.71	(0.59, 0.85)
Air Force Reserve	0.71	(0.64, 0.79)
No military dependents under the age 18 (vs. those with dependents under age 18)	1.02	(0.97, 1.07)

How Results Were Adjusted to Correct for Certain Demographic Subgroups Being More or Less Likely to Participate

As noted within the body, responses in this report were statistically adjusted (*weighted*) to reflect the demographic composition of the Air Force population. Weights account for differences in the characteristics of survey respondents relative to the overall community. Responses were adjusted for these characteristics because they may be related to the survey responses. These adjustments thus protect the results from being distorted by over- or underrepresentation of major subgroups that may have been disproportionately likely or unlikely to participate in the survey. Adjustments can account only for observable characteristics (e.g., gender and pay grade for airmen).

The following characteristics available in Air Force personnel files were used for weighting airmen and civilian employee responses:

- active, guard, or reserve airman or not an airman
- nonappropriated fund civilian employee; appropriated fund civilian employee: General Schedule; appropriated fund civilian employee: Federal Wage System; appropriated fund civilian employee: other; or not an Air Force civilian employee
- gender
- education level
- airmen's pay grade group
- airmen's race and ethnicity
- airmen's career group
- veteran status of civilian employees
- whether airmen had any military dependents under the age 18
- servicing location (installation).

The Air Force personnel files do not contain demographic data on spouses themselves; however, we were able to weight spouses' results to reflect their airmen's characteristics (location, Air Force affiliation [active, guard, reserve], presence of military dependents under age 18).

Recommendations for Administering the Next Community Feedback Tool

Striving for greater lead time between survey approval and survey launch will allow installations more time to promote the survey locally. Some of our participant groups had relatively low numbers participating—most notably, some of the spouse groups. In the process of outreach regarding the survey, Community Support Coordinators noted that they felt that there was relatively little time to get the word out. It is possible that more advance notice would facilitate more interest and move more community members to participate in the survey, particularly given that spouse outreach was relatively light—invitations were sent via one postcard.

We also recommend requesting spouse email addresses from DMDC so that spouses can be sent survey invitations and reminders by email. Greater time would facilitate more than simply marketing; it would facilitate access to additional contact information. Groups for whom we had more-extensive contact information (personnel) had higher participation rates, in part likely because of our ability to contact them somewhat more often to invite them to participate. The survey contained a question about how respondents learned about the survey; preparations for the next survey could include analyzing that question by subgroup, as well as considering the results from the item regarding preferred modes of receiving information from the Air Force about support services.

To address the technological barriers some personnel faced when attempting to access the survey from an Air Force network or computer, avenues to explore would include a phone option for survey participation, the feasibility of both a .com and a .mil route to the survey, and more advanced coordination with SAF/CIO A6 so they can take additional steps to eliminate local filters that may be blocking access.

Relatively few characteristics were significantly associated with differences on the perceived resilience scale, and what differences we found were themselves somewhat small. Furthermore, the average results for airmen were similar to those from the 2013 Air Force Community Assessment Survey (Dixon, 2016). Previously, the 25-item version of this measure administered to enlisted recruits in Air Force basic military training was associated with subsequent attrition from service and a mental health diagnosis within the first six months of service (Bezdjian et al., 2017). Although our analyses of characteristics associated with perceived resilience offered few insights, it is possible that research may reveal value for Air Force headquarters. However, the literature on this measure of resilience suggests that it may not be the best fit for the Air Force population and that, as with other resilience measures, one limitation (among its strengths) is that it lacks the element of context (e.g., how individuals might respond to different types of challenges) (Bezdjian et al., 2017; Dixon, 2016, Dixon and Bares, 2018, Pangallo et al., 2015). The Air Force may want to consider what type of measurement and measure is most suited to their goals for this particular survey (i.e., to provide indicators to community planners rather than data for research) and determine whether adopting or developing alternative measures might be more helpful. For the purposes of this feedback tool, it may be more helpful to focus on the factors that the literature has shown contribute to resilience, such as self-regulation, mastery, social support networks, family communication, problem solving, and positive command climate and on specific types of life stressors rather than on overall, general self-reports of resilience (Bowen and Martin, 2011; Masten, 2015; Meadows et al., 2015; Meredith et al., 2011; Pangallo et al., 2015).

Survey participants who experienced any problems in the past year were asked to indicate what *kinds* of help they or their families needed to deal with the type of problem they had prioritized as most significant or as their only type of problem. Relevant programs and services operating in a resource constrained environment could use the reported associations between top problems and these most pressing needs to focus in on the most frequently paired needs or to consider more broadly the array of needs that community members with a given problem type might be experiencing. This information could be used to inform program planning and outreach efforts. It is worth soliciting feedback regarding the usefulness of this approach from planning teams. A large proportion of respondents reported "other" needs. We could mine these open-ended responses more systematically to determine how many participants were correctly interpreting the question about the general types of needs they experienced in relation to their top problem and how many were using this comment field to restate or further specify their problems, to provide more detail on a need already included on the list, or to jump ahead by referencing the type of resource they needed (e.g., a doctor). We could use this information to consider revisions to the approach taken in this section. The additional effort may be particularly warranted if Community Support Coordinators and leadership do not find the explicit linkage between types of problem and type of respondent-perceived needs to be helpful for planning.

We queried respondents directly about their locations. This facilitated tracking response rates by location during the course of the survey to ensure widespread awareness of and access to the survey. We ultimately used the personnel file's recorded servicing location, however, as the location for both analyses and weighting. Because the list of possible locations is quite long, as shown in Appendix A, it may be worth simplifying the survey for community respondents by relying on personnel data to supply this information wherever possible. The downside to this option would be that it would make it commensurately more difficult to determine response rates for given locations during survey administration.

In consultation with the sponsor, we chose throughout to focus on servicing location rather than on other ways of characterizing location because that location often determines resource planning. However, in a few instances, we were asked during the report preparation stage to consider another method of sorting personnel by location. For example, Community Support Coordinators expressed an interest in seeing separate results for the geographically separated units for which they were responsible because the coordinators anticipated that these locations might have different problems, needs, or challenges accessing resources (e.g., Creech Air Force Base is serviced by Nellis Air Force Base and so was not slated to receive a separate report). Additionally, for some guard wings on active or reserve bases, the bases are the servicing locations; for other guard wings, other in-state guard wings provide services (as is the case with the guard wing on MacDill Air Force Base). Thus, in such cases, base leadership would not have visibility on responses from a tenant guard wing that may also rely on its services for support. Although servicing location seems to be a logical choice, given the purposes of this survey, it may be worth considering whether another method of location assignment is preferable or whether specific exceptions should be planned.

The results of this survey should help identify where content can be trimmed. For example, further exploration of the frequency of individual issues within the problem categories may reveal issues of such low frequency they can be safely omitted for brevity or combined with other issues within the domain. Other areas in the survey may also be considered for trimming. In our survey administration, we tailored the listing for resources to which respondents may have reached out to the type of respondent—for example, only spouses who were not dual-military were asked about whether they reached out to "Other military spouses who are civilians." Ultimately, this tailoring can cause some confusion in reporting results (e.g., some percentages are based on the entire population, some are based on the responses of only certain subgroups) and certainly adds complexity for data end users, who include Air Force personnel.

One challenge was containing the survey length for individuals holding more than one Air Force affiliation, so that the same types of analyses could be done for members of each subgroup. Some respondents are

- airmen and employees
- airmen and spouses of airmen
- employees and spouses of airmen
- airmen, employees, and spouses of airmen.

The more affiliations one holds, the more military service characteristics that could be asked, the longer the lists of possible problems they may have encountered, and the longer the lists of possible military resources they may have contacted. To limit survey length for civilian employees who are also spouses, the 2017 survey asked only about their own employee status and did not also ask about the rank group of their airmen. Current analyses showing that this group of spouses differed from other spouses (e.g., they tended to have higher perceived resilience scores than spouses of junior enlisted personnel did and had greater discomfort using or difficulty finding military resources than spouses of officers and senior NCOs) suggest it would be worth asking Air Force civilian employees who are also spouses to report both their own employment characteristics and their airmen's ranks and components. This would enable the analyses to control for airmen's rank group for all spouses and identify whether spouses who are also civilian employees still differed from their spouse counterparts who are not employees. Alternatively, the Air Force may wish to focus future spouse analyses on spouses who are not also civilian employees so that spouses who are also employees would not need to provide additional information to be included as informatively in the more general spouse analysis.

C. Respondent and Location Characteristics

This section presents weighted information on key respondent characteristics and characteristics of the locations of servicing installations. We provide this only as background information; it was not feasible within the scope of this study to include all these variables in the regression analyses. For the variables that were used in the regression analyses documented in this report, we needed to collapse categories in some cases (e.g., past-year nights away from home, career group) because too few individuals fell into one or more of the options.

Individual and Military Service Characteristics

Airmen

Table C.1 provides demographics from the weighted sample of 56,368 airman survey respondents from across the Air Force. For some key indicators (affiliation, rank group), we relied on personnel records, particularly because we ultimately relied on servicing locations indicated in personnel records for weighting and also for reporting at the installation level. However, survey information was often more detailed—in some cases, providing information not present in personnel records at all and, in other cases, likely to be somewhat more current—so, where, possible we used that information.

Table C.1. Characteristics of Airman Survey Respondents

Characteristic	Data Source	Subgroup	Overall (%)
Affiliation	Personnel files	Active component	64
		Air National Guard	21
		Air Force Reserve	14
Rank group	Personnel files	Enlisted E1–E4	33
		Enlisted E5–E6	30
		Enlisted E7–E9	18
		Officer O1–O3	8
		Officer O4 and above	11
Gender	Survey	Women	21
		Men	79
Race[a]	Survey	White	75
		Black/African American	15
		Other race	18
Ethnicity	Survey	Spanish/Hispanic/Latino	13
Marital status	Survey	Unmarried	25
		Committed relationship	16
		Married	58
		Married to an airman	2
Child status	Survey	Has minor children	47
	Survey	Special needs minor child(ren)	6[b]
Home distance from base	Survey	Lives on base	26
		Lives <30 minutes from base	46
		Lives >30 minutes from base	28
Working somewhere other than a military installation	Survey	Yes (e.g., recruiting station, ROTC, other government agency)	3
Past-year nights away from home	Survey	0–29	63
		30–179	29
		180–365	8
Hours per week working for Air Force duties	Survey	<40	17
		40–49	53
		50–59	22
		60 or more	9
Military career group	Survey	Operations	23
		Logistics/maintenance	31
		Support	28
		Medical	10
		Professional, special investigations, special duty	4
		Acquisition	3
		Other (e.g., training)	1

SOURCE: July 2017 Air Force personnel files and 2017 Air Force Community Feedback Tool responses.
[a] Sums to more than 100% because respondents could choose more than one.
[b] Out of all airman respondents.

Table C.2 provides characteristics of the weighted sample of 27,071 Air Force civilian employee respondents. Employees who are also guard or reserve airmen are represented both Tables C.1 and C.2.

Table C.2. Characteristics of Respondents Who Are Air Force Civilian Employees

Characteristic	Data Source	Subgroup	Overall (%)
Employee type	Personnel files	Nonappropriated Fund	12
		Appropriated fund: General Schedule	53
		Appropriated fund: Federal Wage System	18
		Appropriated fund: Other	17
Dual personnel status	Personnel files	Individual is both guard/reserve and Air Force civilian employee	8
Gender	Survey	Women	34
		Men	66
Race [a]	Survey	White	76
		Black/African American	12
		Other race	15
Ethnicity	Survey	Spanish/Hispanic/Latino	9
Marital status	Survey	Unmarried	16
		Committed relationship	9
		Married	75
Child status	Survey	Has minor children	42
Home distance from base	Survey	Lives on base	4
		Lives <30 minutes from base	67
		Lives >30 minutes from base	29
Hours per week working for Air Force duties	Survey	<40	5
		40–49	82
		50 or more	13
Veteran	Personnel files	Is a military veteran	46

SOURCE: July 2017 Air Force personnel files and 2017 Air Force Community Feedback Tool responses.
[a] NOTE: sums to more than 100% since respondents could choose more than one.

Spouses of Airmen Who are Not Airmen Themselves

Table C.3 provides demographics for the weighted sample of 7,434 respondents who are spouses of airmen but not airmen themselves. Airmen married to other airmen are represented in Table C.1 and are not included in Table C.3.

Table C.3. Characteristics of Spouse Respondents Who Are Not Also Airmen

Characteristic	Data Source	Subgroup	Overall (%)
Affiliation of their airman	Survey	Active component	63
		Air National Guard	23
		Air Force Reserve	14
Rank group of their airman[a]	Survey	Enlisted E1–E4	10
		Enlisted E5–E6	28
		Enlisted E7–E9	19
		Officer O1–O3	12
		Officer O4 and above	20
		Rank group unknown (question not asked)	11
Spouse is also Air Force civilian employee	Survey		11
Spouse education and employment status	Survey	Working full time: typically 35 hours a week or more, including self-employment	33
		Working part time	18
		Unemployed and looking for work	10
		Unemployed and not looking for work	10
		Full-time care of house/children	33
		Full-time student	7
		Part-time student	4
Gender	Survey	Women	92
		Men	8
Race[b]	Survey	White	86
		Black/African American	5
		Other race	13
Ethnicity	Survey	Spanish/Hispanic/Latino	9
Child status	Survey	Has minor children	69
	Survey	Has special needs minor child(ren)	10[c]
Home distance from base	Survey	Lives on base	20
		Lives <30 minutes from base	49
		Lives >30 minutes from base	31
Airman's past-year nights away from home	Survey	0–29	52
		30–179	36
		180–365	11
Airman's hours per week working for Air Force duties	Survey	<40	20
		40–49	41
		50 or more	38

SOURCE: July 2017 Air Force personnel files and 2017 Air Force Community Feedback Tool responses.
[a] Not asked of spouses who are also civilian employees as part of an effort to contain the length of surveys for individuals with multiple Air Force affiliations.
[b] Sums to more than 100% because respondents could choose more than one.
[c] Out of all spouse respondents.

151

Variation in community needs may also be related to location characteristics. For example, Air Force personnel and families located on installations led by other services, in foreign countries, and/or in remote and isolated locations who attempt to access resources may have problems, needs, or experiences that are shaped by the particular circumstances of such settings. Table C.4 shows the location characteristics that we were able to consider in this report for airmen, civilian employees, and spouses of airmen. Note that not all individuals live on or near their servicing locations. For example, personnel could be assigned to geographically separated units; spouses may live somewhere other than their airmen's servicing locations (e.g., during unaccompanied tours); or personnel may have a long commute to their installations or guard wings.

Table C.4. Characteristics of Respondents' Servicing Locations

	Airmen (%)	Civilian Employee (%)	Spouses of Airmen (%)
Foreign country	10	3	10
Remote and isolated[a]	12	8	11
Non–Air Force–led installation	5	3	6
Joint base	17	18	18
Stand-alone guard wing	16	1	17

[a] *Remote and isolated* as defined in AFI 65-106's guidance on the allocation of funds for resources, such as morale, welfare, and recreational programs (AFI 65-106, 2009, p. 14).

D. Specific Issues Experienced Within the Most Commonly Selected Top Problems

This appendix shows the frequency of individual issues within the problems that Air Force community members most frequently selected as either the sole or most significant (*top*) type of problem they experienced in the past year. As described in Chapter 3, the three most common top problem types among both Air Force personnel and spouses of airmen were

- military practices and culture
- own well-being
- work-life balance.

The tables also indicate when certain items were asked only of certain subgroups (e.g., if an item was shown only to guard and reserve respondents or only to spouses). See Appendix B for the complete list of problems within each problem type and which subgroups were shown each.

Air Force Personnel

For each of three problem types Air Force personnel in this community most commonly indicated that they had experienced in the past year, Tables D.1, D.2, and D.3 show how frequently the most common individual problems within those problem types were selected. The tables below reflect items endorsed by at least 20 personnel, although the percentages displayed are based only on responses from airmen or civilian employees for whom one of the three problem types was self-identified as either the sole or most significant type of problem. This information is provided to help the Air Force better tailor its Community Action Plans to the specific types of challenges their personnel have been facing and consider most significant. Note that not all problems are applicable to all subgroups, and percentages are based on the entire Air Force personnel population who selected these as their top types of problems (whether active, guard, or reserve airmen and/or civilian employees).

As shown in Table D.1, 59% of personnel who selected military practices and culture as their top type of past-year problem indicated that one of the specific problems was poor leadership by the military chain of command. Table D.2 shows that sleeping problems, fatigue, and stress were each reported by about 50% of personnel who selected their own well-being as their top type of past-year problem. Relatedly, in Table D.3 we see that, among personnel for whom work-life balance was their top type of problem, the most commonly reported specific problems were finding enough time for sleep, a healthy diet, or physical exercise (62%); finding time for recreation, stress relief, or family (59%); and many competing commitments, such as work, school, and childcare (57%).

Table D.1. Air Force Personnel Who Experienced Different
***Military Practices and Culture* Problems in the Past Year**

Individual Problem	%
Poor leadership by military personnel in your chain of command [asked only of personnel]	59
Lack of support for your professional/career development [asked only of personnel]	41
Poor relationship with coworkers or superiors [asked only of personnel]	36
Poor leadership by civilian personnel in your chain of command [asked only of personnel]	33
Getting Air Force personnel to listen to you, take you seriously, or treat you with respect	33
Not being able to stay at or go to the military installation you prefer	20
Getting accurate information about when you will have to move, deploy, or travel for work [asked only of airmen not married to military personnel and employees not married to airmen]	19
Inequity regarding bonuses/raises/promotions [asked only of employees]	13
Military leadership not understanding the civilian workforce [asked only of employees]	11
Military coworkers not valuing civilian workforce contributions [asked only of employees]	8
Difficulty finding a good Air Force or Department of Defense job [asked only of employees]	6
Your spouse or partner's adjustment to military culture [asked only of personnel]	6
Adjusting to military language, organization, or culture	6
Being able to balance civilian employment with your guard and reserve duties [asked only of guard and reserve]	5
Having to use annual leave to participate in unit social activities [asked only of employees]	5
Problems with requests for reasonable workplace accommodations for your disability [asked only of employees]	1
Leadership not understanding the needs of dual military couples [asked only of those in dual military marriages]	1
Getting accurate information about when you or your spouse will have to move, deploy, or travel for work [asked only of those in dual military marriages]	1
Lack of contact with other military spouses [asked only of spouses]	<1
Getting accurate information about when your spouse will have to move, deploy, or travel for work [asked only of spouses]	<1
Civilian leadership not understanding military spouses [asked only of employees who are also military spouses]	<1
Other military spouses not treating you with respect [asked only of spouses]	<1

NOTES: N = 19,604. Responses to items shown only to spouses appear in this personnel table only if those spouses were also civilian employees.

154

Table D.2. Air Force Personnel Who Experienced Different
Own Well-Being Problems in the Past Year

Individual Problem	%
Sleeping problems (too little or too much, nightmares, etc.)	53
Frequently tired	51
Feeling stressed or overwhelmed	50
Managing your weight	42
Mood: depression, impatience, anger, aggression, anxiety	40
Pain, physical injury, or illness	39
Hard to focus, concentrate, or remember things	37
Loneliness or boredom	30
Work not challenging or doesn't use your skills/education	22
Difficulty finding meaning or purpose in life	20
Grieving the loss of a friend or loved one	17
Too much time playing video games, watching TV or movies, or using the Internet or social media (Facebook, Twitter, Snapchat, etc.)	15
Difficulty controlling your spending	10
Doing poorly in school or work	8
Challenges due to your physical or learning disability	5
Substance misuse or abuse (alcohol, tobacco, drugs)	4
Adapting to living in a foreign country	3

NOTES: *N* = 13,846

Table D.3. Air Force Personnel Who Experienced Different
***Work-Life Balance* Problems in the Past Year**

Individual Problem	%
Finding time for enough sleep, a healthy diet, or physical exercise	62
Finding time for recreation, stress relief, or family time	59
Many competing commitments (such as work, school, childcare, volunteer activities)	57
Finding time to pursue your education	44
Finding time for social activities outside of work	43
Work hours, schedule, or commute to your military job [asked only of airmen]	39
Lack of opportunities for telework or alternative work schedule [asked only of employees]	8
Work hours, schedule, or commute to your civilian job [asked only of guard and reserve]	7
Work hours, schedule, or commute to work [asked only of employees and spouses]	7
Getting permission or having to take leave to take care of important errands during the work day [asked only of employees]	4

NOTES: N = 13,395

Spouses of Airmen

For three specified problem types that spouses of airmen most commonly indicated that they had experienced in the past year, this section shows how frequently the most common individual problems within those problem types were selected. The tables that follow reflect items endorsed by at least 20 spouses, although the percentages displayed are based only on responses from spouses of airmen who are not airmen themselves and for whom one of the problem types was self-identified as either the sole or most significant type of problem.

The tables include items that were asked only of spouses who are also civilian employees because the items were intended to provide insights into their Air Force employment. Spouses who are not civilian employees may encounter similar challenges in their jobs, but these employment conditions are outside the purview of the Air Force. Therefore, to limit survey length, specific job-related items were not asked of all spouses.

As shown in Table D.4, among spouses who selected their own well-being as their top type of past-year problem, the most frequently reported issues were stress (61%), fatigue (51%), managing weight (50%) and mood (e.g., depression, anger) (48%). Table D.5 shows that, among spouses for whom work-life balance was their top type of problem, the most commonly reported issues were finding enough time for recreation, stress relief, or family (62%); finding time for a healthy diet or physical exercise (62%); and many competing commitments, such as work, school and childcare (60%). Among spouses for whom military practices and culture was their top type of past-year problem, the most commonly selected issue was getting accurate information about when their airmen will have to move, deploy, or travel for work (46%).

Table D.4. Spouses Who Experienced Different
***Own Well-Being* Problems in the Past Year**

Individual Problem	%
Feeling stressed or overwhelmed	61
Frequently tired	51
Managing your weight	50
Mood: depression, impatience, anger, aggression, anxiety	48
Sleeping problems (too little or too much, nightmares, etc.)	43
Loneliness or boredom	41
Hard to focus, concentrate, or remember things	30
Pain, physical injury, or illness	24
Too much time playing video games, watching TV or movies, or using the Internet or social media (Facebook, Twitter, Snapchat, etc.)	22
Difficulty finding meaning or purpose in life	21
Grieving the loss of a friend or loved one	17
Work not challenging or doesn't use your skills/education	16
Difficulty controlling your spending	9
Adapting to living in a foreign country	5
Challenges due to your physical or learning disability	4
Doing poorly in school or work	3
Substance misuse or abuse (alcohol, tobacco, drugs)	3

NOTES: *N* = 1,356

Table D.5. Spouses Who Experienced Different
***Work-Life Balance* Problems in the Past Year**

Individual Problem	%
Finding time for recreation, stress relief, or family time	62
Finding time for enough sleep, a healthy diet, or physical exercise	62
Many competing commitments (such as work, school, childcare, volunteer activities)	60
Work hours, schedule, or commute to work [asked only of employees and spouses]	42
Finding time for social activities outside of work	33
Finding time to pursue your education	24
Lack of opportunities for telework or alternative work schedule [asked only of employees]	5
Getting permission or having to take leave to take care of important errands during the work day [asked only of employees]	4

NOTES: *N* = 960.

Table D.6. Spouses Who Experienced Different
***Military Practices and Culture* Problems in the Past Year**

Individual Problem	%
Getting accurate information about when your spouse will have to move, deploy, or travel for work [asked only of spouses]	46
Lack of contact with other military spouses [asked only of spouses]	33
Not being able to stay at or go to the military installation you prefer	28
Adjusting to military language, organization, or culture	19
Getting Air Force personnel to listen to you, take you seriously, or treat you with respect	18
Poor leadership by civilian personnel in your chain of command [asked only of personnel]	15
Civilian leadership not understanding military spouses [asked only of employees who are also military spouses]	13
Lack of support for your professional/career development [asked only of personnel]	13
Difficulty finding a good Air Force or Department of Defense job [asked only of employees]	12
Other military spouses not treating you with respect [asked only of spouses]	12
Poor leadership by military personnel in your chain of command [asked only of personnel]	11
Military leadership not understanding the civilian workforce [asked only of employees]	11
Inequity regarding bonuses/raises/promotions [asked only of employees]	9
Having to use annual leave to participate in unit social activities [asked only of employees]	9
Poor relationship with coworkers or superiors [asked only of personnel]	9
Military coworkers not valuing civilian workforce contributions [asked only of employees]	9
Getting accurate information about when you or your spouse will have to move, deploy, or travel for work [asked only of those in dual military marriages]	1

NOTES: *N* = 926.

E. Integrated Health Summary

This appendix brings together overall highlights of the health and health care–related findings that are reported in various places in the body of this report.

Perceptions of Well-Being

More than 55% of community members believed that their health is excellent or very good, and only 1–2% rated it as poor. On average, the number of self-reported poor physical health days in the past month was 3.9 among Air Force personnel and 3.3 among spouses of airmen; the average number of self-reported poor mental health days in the past month was 3.4 among Air Force personnel and 4.5 among spouses of airmen.

Community members reported that poor mental or physical health had kept them from their usual activities, such as self-care, work, or recreation, for about two to three days in the past month. Among airmen, working less than 40 hours a week, living on base, serving in the guard or reserve, and being a senior officer were typically among the characteristics associated with about one less limited-activity day in the past month, compared with other subgroups of airmen. Among spouses, being married to a junior or senior officer, having children, and being employed or self-employed were associated with about one less limited-activity day. Civilian employees did not differ in this regard by demographic or military service characteristics. None of the community members' self-reported limited-activity days that were due to poor health varied notably by location type (i.e., remote and isolated, in a foreign country, an installation not led by the Air Force, or somewhere other than a military installation, such an ROTC or recruiting unit).

Turning to the measure of perceived resilience, 2017 scores within the Air Force community were similar to scores in the general population and varied very little across demographic subgroups. Out of a highest possible perceived resilience score of 40, Air Force personnel had an average score of 31.8, and spouses had an average score of 29.6. There is no standard set of discrete cutoff scores that distinguish vulnerable from resilient populations.

Well-Being Problems

Across all personnel, problems with their own well-being in the past year were among the most common: 65% of Air Force personnel and 73% of spouses encountered such problems. 20% of Air Force personnel and spouses reported that issues with their own well-being were their top past-year problem. Of this population, 25% of Air Force personnel and 22% of spouses said that at their worst, their own well-being problems became severe. About 50% of personnel for whom their own well-being was their top type of past-year problem reported each of the following issues: sleeping problems, fatigue, and stress. Stress, fatigue, managing weight, and

159

mood (e.g., depression, anger) were each the issues most commonly reported by spouses for whom well-being was their top problem in the past year (61% reported stress, about 50% reported the other issues).

Problems do not necessary result in needs for assistance: 43% of personnel and 38% of spouses for whom their own well-being was their top past-year problem did not believe they had any need for assistance to deal with these problems. However, the following needs were perceived by community members with own well-being as their top problem:

- 17% of personnel and 25% of spouses needed emotional or social support.
- 15% of personnel and 17% of spouses felt they needed professional counseling.
- 14% of personnel and 19% of spouses believed they needed activities or facilities for fitness, recreation, stress relief, or family bonding.
- 14% of personnel and 10% of spouses perceived a need for advice, coaching, or education to help them.

Health Care System Problems

At the time of the survey, 37% of Air Force personnel and 38% of spouses had faced problems with the health care system in the past year: 7% of personnel and 12% of spouses said these were their sole or most significant problems in the past year. Among these community members, 25 to 26% said the problem was severe at its worst.

Across the Air Force community, 18% of personnel and 19% of spouses believed that the wait list or response times for military medical and health care providers is too long, and 41% of personnel and 33% of spouses said these providers have a good reputation.

Regarding military mental health care providers, only 4% of personnel and spouses felt the wait list or response time was too long, and 39% of personnel and 21% of spouses felt these providers had a good reputation.

However, 14% of personnel and 26% spouses felt they knew little to nothing about military medical and health care providers, and 25% of personnel and 52% of spouses knew little to nothing about military mental health care providers.

Among those who believed they had any needs for their top past-year problem (regardless of what that problem was), mental health care providers (as well as religious or spiritual resources) were among those with the highest percentage of personnel and spouses feeling that they helped "a lot" with their greatest needs: 30 to 32% of personnel and spouses felt this way about mental health care providers. In contrast, 17 to 18% of personnel and spouses who turned to medical and health care providers for assistance believed that these providers helped a lot. Among those who turned to a private medical provider not paid for by the military or to a private mental health care provider not paid for by the military, 32 to 34% of personnel and spouses felt these nonmilitary resources helped a lot with their needs.

Across the ratings of military resources, among the highest were ratings for support services for victims of violence: 50% of personnel and 24% of spouses believed these services collectively have a good reputation, and only 1% of personnel and spouses believed these services have a wait list or response time that is too long. However, 20% of personnel and 60% of spouses reported knowing little to nothing about them. Given that one of these services is the Family Advocacy Program, designed to address domestic violence and child abuse and neglect, this finding suggests that efforts are needed to raise awareness of the program among spouses in particular.

References

AFI—*See* Air Force Instruction.

Air Force Instruction 65-106, *Appropriated Fund Support of Morale, Welfare, and Recreation (MWR) and Nonappropriated Fund Instrumentalities (NAFIS)*, May 6, 2009.

Air Force Instruction 90-501, *Community Action Information Board (CAIB) and Integrated Delivery System (IDS)*, October 15, 2013, Incorporating Change 1, August 14, 2014.

Air Force Instruction 90-506, *Comprehensive Airman Fitness*, April 2, 2014.

Air Force Personnel Center, "Demographics," June 30, 2018a. As of September 20, 2018: https://www.afpc.af.mil/About/Air-Force-Demographics/

Air Force Personnel Center, *Airman and Family Readiness Center Key Spouse Program: Key Spouse Guide*, May 2018b. As of April 11, 2019: https://www.afpc.af.mil/LinkClick.aspx?fileticket=lIP0glG_p50%3D&portalid=70

Ausink, John A., Miriam Matthews, Raymond E. Conley, and Nelson Lim, *Improving the Effectiveness of Air Force Squadron Commanders: Assessing Squadron Commander Responsibilities, Preparation, and Resources,* Santa Monica, Calif.: RAND Corporation, RR-2233-AF, 2018. As of April 11, 2019: https://www.rand.org/pubs/research_reports/RR2233.html

Bezdjian, Serena, Kristin G. Schneider, Danielle Burchett, Monty T. Baker, and Howard N. Garb, "Resilience in the United States Air Force: Psychometric Properties of the Connor-Davidson Resilience Scale (CD-RISC)," *Psychological Assessment*, Vol. 29, No. 5, 2017, pp. 479-485.

Booth, Bradford, Mady Wechsler Segal, and D. Bruce Bell, *What We Know About Army Families: 2007 Update*, Ft. Belvoir, Va.: Family and Morale, Welfare and Recreation Command, 2007.

Bowen, Gary L., and James A. Martin, "The Resiliency Model of Role Performance for Service Members, Veterans, and their Families: A Focus on Social Connections and Individual Assets," *Journal of Human Behavior in the Social Environment*, Vol. 21, No. 2, March 2011, pp. 162–178.

Brown, Ryan Andrew, Grant N. Marshall, Joshua Breslau, Coreen Farris, Karen Chan Osilla, Harold Alan Pincus, Teague Ruder, Phoenix Voorhies, Dionne Barnes-Proby, Katherine Pfrommer, Lisa Miyashiro, Yashodhara Rana, and David M. Adamson, *Access to Behavioral Health Care for Geographically Remote Service Members and Dependents in the U.S.,* Santa

Monica, Calif.: RAND Corporation, RR-578-OSD, 2015. As of April 11, 2019:
https://www.rand.org/pubs/research_reports/RR578.html

Burnam, M. Audrey, Lisa S. Meredith, Cathy D. Sherbourne, Robert B. Valdez, and Georges Vernez, *Army Families and Soldier Readiness*. Santa Monica, Calif.: RAND Corporation, R-3884-A, 1992. As of February 1, 2012:
http://www.rand.org/pubs/reports/R3884.html

Campbell, Amy, Joe Luchman, and James Khun, *Spousal Support to Stay as a Predictor of Actual Retention Behavior: A Logistic Regression Analysis*, Alexandria, Va.: Defense Research, Surveys, and Statistics Center, Office of People Analytics, Survey Note 2017-009, 2017.

Campbell-Sills, Laura, David R. Forde, and Murray B. Stein, "Demographic and Childhood Environmental Predictors of Resilience in a Community Sample," *Journal of Psychiatric Research,* Vol. 43, No. 12, August 2009, pp. 1007–1012.

CD-RISC—*See* Connor-Davidson Resilience Scale.

Centers for Disease Control and Prevention, *Health-Related Quality of Life (HRQOL)*, May 26, 2016. As of September 7, 2017:
https://www.cdc.gov/hrqol/hrqol14_measure.htm

Cohen, Jacob, *Statistical Power Analysis for the Behavioral Sciences*, 2nd ed., Hillsdale, N.J.: Erlbaum, 1988.

Cole, Stephen R., and Miguel A. Hernán, "Constructing Inverse Probability Weights for Marginal Structural Models," *American Journal of Epidemiology*, Vol. 168, No. 6, 2008, pp. 656–664.

Connor-Davidson Resilience Scale website, undated. As of April 25, 2019:
http://www.cd-risc.com/index.php

Connor, Kathryn M., and Jonathan R.T. Davidson, "Development of a New Resilience Scale: The Connor-Davidson Resilience Scale (CD-RISC)," *Depression and Anxiety*, Vol. 18, No. 2, 2003, pp. 76–82.

Department of Defense Instruction 3216.02, *Protection of Human Subjects and Adherence to Ethical Standards in DoD-Supported Research,* Washington, D.C., November 8, 2011, Incorporating Change 1, October 15, 2018.

Dixon, Mark A., *Deployment Resilience Among U.S. Airmen: A Secondary Analysis of Risk and Protective Factors Using the 2013 Community Assessment Survey*, dissertation, Richmond, Va.: Virginia Commonwealth University, 2016.

Dixon, Mark A., and Cristina B. Bares, "Resilience in the U.S. Air Force: A Factor Analysis of Two Resilience Scales," *Military Behavioral Health,* Vol. 6, No. 1, 2018, pp. 41–49.

GAO—*See* U.S. Government Accountability Office.

Grattan, Lynn M., Sparkle Roberts, William T. Mahan, Patrick K. McLaughlin, W. Steven Otwell, and J. Glenn Morris, "The Early Psychological Impacts of the Deepwater Horizon Oil Spill on Florida and Alabama Communities," *Environmental Health Perspectives*, Vol. 119, No. 6, February 2011, pp. 838–843.

Griffeth, Roger W., Peter W. Hom, and Stefan Gaertner, "A Meta-Analysis of Antecedents and Correlates of Employee Turnover: Update, Moderator Tests, and Research Implications for the Next Millennium," *Journal of Management*, Vol. 26, No. 3, June 2000, pp. 463–488.

Groves, Robert M., "Nonresponse Rates and Nonresponse Bias in Household Surveys," *Public Opinion Quarterly,* Vol. 70, No. 5, 2006, pp. 646–675.

Groves, Robert M., and Emilia Peytcheva, "The Impact of Nonresponse Rates on Nonresponse Bias: A Meta-Analysis," *Public Opinion Quarterly*, Vol. 72, No. 2, 2008, pp. 167–189.

Hom, Peter, and Rodger Griffeth, *Employee Turnover*, Cincinnati, Ohio: South-Western Publishers, 1995.

Johnson, Timothy P., and Joseph S. Wislar, "Response Rates and Nonresponse Errors in Surveys," *Journal of the American Medical Association,* Vol. 307, No. 17, May 2, 2012, pp. 1805–1806.

Lino, Mark, Kevin Kuczynski, Nestor Rodriquez, and TusaRebecca Schap, *Expenditures on Children by Families, 2015*, Washington, D.C.: U.S. Department of Agriculture, Center for Nutrition Policy and Promotion, Miscellaneous Publication No. 1528-2015, March 2017. As of August 7, 2019:
https://www.cnpp.usda.gov/sites/default/files/crc2015_March2017.pdf

Masten, Ann S., "Pathways to Integrated Resilience Science," *Psychological Inquiry: An International Journal for the Advancement of Psychological Theory*, Vol. 26, No. 2, June 2015, pp. 187–196.

McCanlies, Eric C., Anna Mnatsakanova, Michael E. Andrew, Cecil M. Burchfield, and John M. Violanti, "Positive Psychological Factors Are Associated with Lower PTSD Symptoms Among Police Officers: Post Hurricane Katrina," *Stress and Health*, Vol. 30, No. 5, December 2014, pp. 405–415.

Meadows, Sarah O., Megan K. Beckett, Kirby Bowling, Daniela Golinelli, Michael P. Fisher, Laurie T. Martin, Lisa S. Meredith, and Karen Chan Osilla, *Family Resilience in the Military: Definitions, Models and Policies*, Santa Monica, Calif.: RAND Corporation,

RR-470-OSD, 2015. As of April 11, 2019:
https://www.rand.org/pubs/research_reports/RR470.html

Meadows, Sarah O., Charles C. Engel, Rebecca L. Collins, Robin L. Beckman, Matthew Cefalu, Jennifer Hawes-Dawson, Molly Doyle, Amii M. Kress, Lisa Sontag-Padilla, Rajeev Ramchand, and Kayla M. Williams, *2015 Department of Defense Health Related Behaviors Survey (HRBS)*, Santa Monica, Calif.: RAND Corporation, RR-1695-OSD, 2018. As of April 11, 2019:
https://www.rand.org/pubs/research_reports/RR1695.html

Meadows, Sarah O., Laura L. Miller, and Sean Robson, *Airman and Family Resilience: Lessons from the Scientific Literature*, Santa Monica, Calif.: RAND Corporation, RR-106-AF, 2015. As of April 11, 2019:
https://www.rand.org/pubs/research_reports/RR106.html

Melvin, Kristal C., Deborah Gross, Matthew J. Hayat, Bonnie Mowinski Jennings, and Jacquelyn C. Campbell, "Couple Functioning and Post-Traumatic Stress Symptoms in US Army Couples: The Role of Resilience," *Research in Nursing & Health*, Vol. 35, No. 2, April 2012, pp. 164–177.

Meredith, Lisa S., Cathy D. Sherbourne, Sarah Gaillot, Lydia Hansell, Hans V. Ritschard, Andrew M. Parker, and Glenda Wrenn, *Promoting Psychological Resilience in the U.S. Military*, Santa Monica, Calif.: RAND Corporation, MG-996-OSD, 2011. As of April 11, 2019:
https://www.rand.org/pubs/monographs/MG996.html

Miller, Laura L., and Eyal Aharoni, *Understanding Low Survey Response Rates Among Young U.S. Military Personnel*, RAND Corporation, RR-881-AF, 2015. As of June 28, 2019:
https://www.rand.org/pubs/research_reports/RR881.html

Miller, Laura L., Bernard D. Rostker, Rachel M. Burns, Dionne Barnes-Proby, Sandraluz Lara-Cinisomo, and Terry R. West, *A New Approach for Assessing the Needs of Service Members and Their Families*, Santa Monica, Calif.: RAND Corporation, MG-1124-OSD, 2011. As of January 12, 2018:
https://www.rand.org/pubs/monographs/MG1124.html

National Research Council, Division of Behavioral and Social Sciences and Education, Committee on National Statistics, Panel on the Research Agenda for the Future of Social Science Data Collection, *Nonresponse in Social Science Surveys: A Research Agenda*, Roger Tourangeau and Thomas J. Plewes, eds., Washington, D.C.: National Academies Press, 2013.

Office of People Analytics, *2017 Status of Forces Survey of Active Duty Members: Tabulations of Responses*, Alexandria, Va., 2018a.

Office of People Analytics, *2017 Survey of Active Duty Spouses: Tabulations of Responses*, Alexandria, Va., 2018b.

Office of People Analytics, *2017 Status of Forces Survey of Reserve Component Members: Tabulations of Responses*, Alexandria, Va., 2018c.

Office of People Analytics, *2017 Status of Forces Survey of Reserve Component Spouses: Tabulations of Responses*, Alexandria, Va., 2018d.

Office of People Analytics, *Response Rates: Recommended Strategies for Improvement,* Alexandria, Va., Survey Note 2018-071, 2018e.

OPA—*See* Office of People Analytics.

Pangallo, Antonio, Lara Zibarras, Rachel Lewis, and Paul Flaxman, "Resilience Through the Lens of Interactionism: A Systematic Review," *Psychological Assessment,* Vol. 27, No. 1, March 2015.

Pittman, Joe F., Jennifer L. Kerpelman, and Jennifer M. McFadyen, "Internal and External Adaptation in Army Families: Lessons from Operations Desert Shield and Desert Storm," *Family Relations,* Vol. 53, No. 3, 2004, pp. 249–260.

Rainey, Evan E., Laura Petrey, Magan Colleen Reynolds, Stephanie Agtarap, and Ann Marie Warren, "Psychological Factors Predicting Outcome After Traumatic Injury: The Role of Resilience," *Journal of American Surgery,* Vol. 208, No. 4, October 2014.

RAND Corporation, "2017 Air Force Community Feedback Tool," webpage, 2017. As of April 30, 2019:
https://www.rand.org/surveys/af-feedback.html

Segal, Mady Wechsler, and Jesse J. Harris, *What We Know About Army Families*, Alexandria, Va.: U.S. Army Research Institute for the Behavioral and Social Sciences, 1993.

Sims, Carra S., Thomas E. Trail, Emily K. Chen, Erika Mesa, Parisa Roshan, and Beth E. Lachman, *Assessing the Needs of Soldiers and Their Families at the Garrison Level*, Santa Monica, Calif.: RAND Corporation, RR-2148-A, 2018. As of April 11, 2019:
https://www.rand.org/pubs/research_reports/RR2148.html

Sims, Carra S., Thomas E. Trail, Emily K. Chen, and Laura L. Miller, *Today's Soldier: Assessing the Needs of Soldiers and Their Families*, Santa Monica, Calif.: RAND Corporation, RR-1893-A, 2017. As of April 11, 2019:
https://www.rand.org/pubs/research_reports/RR1893.html

Skinner, C.J., and J. D'Arrigo, "Inverse Probability Weighting for Clustered Nonresponse," *Biometrika,* Vol. 98, No. 4, December 2011, pp. 953–966.

Troxel, Wendy M., Regina A. Shih, Eric Pedersen, Lily Geyer, Michael P. Fisher, Beth Ann Griffin, Ann C. Haas, Jeremy R. Kurz, and Paul S. Steinberg, *Sleep in the Military: Promoting Healthy Sleep Among U.S, Servicemembers,* Santa Monica, Calif.: RAND Corporation, RR-739-OSD, 2015. As of April 11, 2019: https://www.rand.org/pubs/research_reports/RR739.html

United Health Foundation, "Poor Physical Health Days in United States in 2017," America's Health Rankings website, 2018a. As of March 11, 2019: https://www.americashealthrankings.org/explore/annual/measure/PhysicalHealth/state/ALL

United Health Foundation, "Poor Mental Health Days in United States in 2017," America's Health Rankings website, 2018b. As of March 11, 2019: https://www.americashealthrankings.org/explore/annual/measure/MentalHealth/state/ALL

U.S. Air Force, *Air Force Enlisted Classification Directory,* April 30, 2015.

U.S. Air Force, "Community Feedback Survey," in *Around the Air Force: Irma Prep/Fighter Crew Retention*, video, Air Force TV, September 7, 2017. As of April 30, 2019: https://www.youtube.com/watch?v=NglPChRFKIk

U.S. Government Accountability Office, *Human Capital: Quality of DOD Status of Forces Surveys Could Be Improved by Performing Nonresponse Analysis of the Results,* Washington, D.C., GAO-10-751R, July 12, 2010.

U.S. Government Accountability Office, *Principles of Federal Appropriations Law Chapter 3, Availability of Appropriations: Purpose*, Washington, D.C., GAO-17-797SP, 2017.

Wasserstein, Ronald L., and Nicole A. Lazar, "The ASA's Statement on *p*-Values: Context, Process and Purpose," *American Statistician*, Vol. 70, No. 2, 2016, pp. 129–133. As of July 18, 2018: https://doi.org/10.1080/00031305.2016.1154108

Watson, Nathaniel F., M. Safwan Badr, Gregory Belenky, Donald L. Bliwise, Orfeu M. Buxton, Daniel Buysse, David F. Dinges, James Gangwisch, Michael A. Grandner, Clete Kushida, Raman K. Malhotra, Jennifer L. Martin, Sanjay R. Patel, Stuart F. Quan, and Esra Tasali, "Recommended Amount of Sleep for a Healthy Adult: A Joint Consensus Statement of the American Academy of Sleep Medicine and Sleep Research Society," *Sleep*, Vol. 38, No. 6, June 2015, pp. 843–844.